Barnsley FC's Greatest Games

Tommy Taylor: one of Barnsley's greatest players. Arthur Bower

Barnsley Football Club's Greatest Games

1890s–2008

Grenville Firth

First published in Great Britain in 2009 by
Wharncliffe Books
an imprint of
Pen and Sword Books Limited,
47 Church Street, Barnsley,
South Yorkshire S70 2AS

Copyright © Grenville Firth, 2009

ISBN: 978 1 84563 1 062

Printed and bound in Great Britain by CPI UK

Pen & Sword Books Ltd incorporates the imprints of
Pen & Sword Aviation, Pen & Sword Maritime,
Pen & Sword Military, Wharncliffe Local History, Pen & Sword Select,
Pen & Sword Military Classics, Leo Cooper, Remember When,
Seaforth Publishing and Frontline Publishing

For a complete list of Pen & Sword titles please contact:
PEN & SWORD BOOKS LIMITED
47 Church Street, Barnsley, South Yorkshire, S70 2AS, England.
E-mail: enquiries@pen-and-sword.co.uk
Website: www.pen-and-sword.co.uk

Foreword

I was born and bred in Glasgow, and learned my trade as a professional footballer under some excellent coaches and managers.

The first person in football to make a big impact on me was Davie McParlin. He started as my coach, and then became manager at Partick Thistle. He was a father-type of figure who educated and prepared me and gave me an excellent foundation for the professional game.

I was then transferred to Celtic and worked under the great Jock Stein. Nothing I can say in words can convey the genius of the man. I feel very privileged to have played for such an icon of the modern game. The way he thought about the game, reacted to situations, and the passion he held for football was an education for everyone associated with him.

Then came my signing for Barnsley by Allan Clarke. Allan went on to sign a number of good players, and the club was playing some of the best football in its history. Big games were coming thick and fast, and I was beginning to see just how special the club, the fans and the town were. At one stage, I believe we had the highest home support in the league. Every week we had an extra man on the field, in the shape of our noisy, chanting, encouraging fans.

We claimed victories at Sheffield Wednesday, Sheffield United, Leeds and Newcastle, and were a force to be reckoned with no matter where we went. We had a wonderful team which just gelled and complimented each other. We felt, as a team, almost invincible at times.

I still recall all our games very clearly, but the one that really stands out in my memory, is when we played Fulham at Oakwell. After fifteen minutes we were 3–0 down, going nowhere fast. In fact, in the next fifteen minutes, we could easily have been 6–0 down. Still, we stuck doggedly to our task, gradually clawing our way back into the game and Ian Banks scored just before half-time to give us a glimmer of hope. In the second half, we chased everything and everyone. The crowd kicked in, cheering every pass, every move we made. It took another twenty minutes before Banks scored with another of his trademark 'specials' which gave us real hope. A couple of minutes later, the goalkeeper fumbled a shot and I happened to be on hand to tap in the equaliser. The atmosphere was electric, the crowd never stopped, the noise was deafening. Tony Cunningham then got his head to a cross to make it 4–3 and Oakwell erupted. That was the final score, and I recall coming off the field applauding the fans. I truly believe without them, we would have lost that game.

In my career, I have been very fortunate to have played in several Cup Finals and Championship Title games and many other big matches with both Partick Thistle and Celtic, but the Fulham game really does stand out in my memory above all the others.

I would like to take the opportunity to say Thank You to the many fans who supported me and my team mates during a very special time in my career, something I will never forget, and am sure all the games that Grenville has selected will make compelling reading.

Ronnie Glavin
2009

Introduction

Since I wrote *Oakwell. The Official History of Barnsley Football Club* in 1978, there have been numerous books on the club, but to my knowledge none that have covered specific matches in any depth.

Having to select just over fifty matches from over 4,600 games that the club have played during their long history has not been easy. Some games are clearly a must, such as the two FA Cup Finals, Semi-Finals, the Wembley experiences and the Millennium Stadium.

For someone who has been lucky enough to see more than 800 Barnsley games, there are many imprinted on one's mind and some of those are included here. Indeed since the 1950/51 season, when I can first recall seeing the Reds in action, of the 34 games listed from this date, I have been fortunate to have watched 28 of them.

What makes a game 'Great?' Is it the fact that the result caused a major FA Cup upset or earned the club promotion or enabled them to avoid relegation? Or is it a spectacular score-line? Or the individual skill or brilliance of a Reds favourite, such as Frank Eaton's first ever five goals in one match or Tommy Taylor's hat-trick in only his second game for the club? The skill and courage that the team displayed in a game that they did not necessarily win, but in which they showed all of these qualities that years later still warms the heart.

I have endeavoured to include a variety of games, spanning the entire history of the club from its origins as Barnsley St Peter's to the present, a period in excess of 120 years. Also I have tried to ensure that the sequence of matches covers the fluctuating fortunes it has endured throughout its existence.

My own favourites include the 5–4 win over Sheffield Wednesday, Arthur Kaye's brilliant individual performance against Ipswich, the best I can recall in a Reds shirt, the amazing Brighton cup tie, the FA Cup ties of 1960/61, likewise the League Cup games of 1981/82, the Wembley experiences and finally and not least, the never to be forgotten Bradford City game which enabled the Reds to reach the pinnacle of English Football.

Apart from the actual report of the game, I have included in some reports, post-match comments from managers and players. In the early days of the Reds history, I have written as reported, to highlight the style of writing in those days and also the football terminology used such as 'custodian' for goalkeeper and 'leather' and 'sphere' for ball.

There are so many unforgettable games that many of you when you have finished reading the book, will say, why did he omit this game or that game?

I hope you derive as much pleasure from reading Barnsley's 'Greatest Games' as I have done from researching and writing it, and hope that, as the book is being read, more 'Great' games will be played by a club that has thrilled us again and again over the years.

Grenville Firth
May 2009

Acknowledgements

I would like to thank Arthur Bower and David Wood for their assistance and comments; and also the sports writers and photographers of the following newspapers:

Barnsley Chronicle, *Barnsley Independent*, *Sheffield Telegraph* and *Star*, the *Green Un*, and the *Yorkshire Post*, most notably Stan Bulmer (Stan Plus Two), John Culley, Jim Ferguson, Benny Hill, Andrew Lodge, Keith Lodge, Trevor Lovett, Simon Meeks, Brian Steer, Keith Turner and John Uprichard.

Also to the reporters of the bygone days of the *Barnsley Chronicle*, *Barnsley Independent*, and *Sheffield Telegraph*, who often wrote under various pseudonyms which included the names 'centre forward' and 'looker on'.

Finally and not least to Ronnie Glavin for providing the Foreword and reminding us all of one of the best periods in the club's history.

Many of the photographs, especially the early ones, are from my own collection, accumulated over many years. However, picture credits, where a source is known, have been placed after captions. Whilst every attempt has been made to acknowledge the original source of copyright for all pictures in this book, if anyone has any questions relating to this matter please contact me via the Publishers.

'Amos', Barnsley's famous FA Cup mascot, outside the club headquarters
(The Clarence Hotel) in c.1908. Brian Elliott

Contents

Barnsley's Greatest Games

1	2 February 1895	Barnsley St Peter's 1 Liverpool 2 FA Cup 1st Round
2	1 September 1898	Lincoln City 1 Barnsley 0 Football League Second Division
3	20 January 1910	Barnsley 6 Blackpool 0 FA Cup 1st Round Replay
4	5 March 1910	Barnsley 1 Queens Park Rangers 0 FA Cup 4th Round
5	31 March 1910	Barnsley 3 Everton 0 FA Cup Semi-Final Replay
6	23 April 1910	Barnsley 1 Newcastle United 1 FA Cup Final
7	21 March 1912	Barnsley 3 Bradford City 2 FA Cup Fourth Round, 3rd Replay
8	3 April 1912	Barnsley 1 Swindon Town 0 FA Cup Semi-Final Replay
9	24 April 1912	Barnsley 1 West Bromwich Albion 0 FA Cup Final Replay
10	6 March 1920	Barnsley 4 Fulham 1 Football League Second Division
11	9 April 1927	Barnsley 6 South Shields 1 Football League Second Division
12	24 January 1931	Barnsley 2 Sheffield Wednesday 1 FA Cup Fourth Round
13	12 December 1932	Barnsley 7 Crewe Alexandra 1 Football League Third Division North
14	3 February 1934	Accrington Stanley 0 Barnsley 9 Football League Third Division North
15	5 May 1934	New Brighton 0 Barnsley 1 Football League Third Division North
16	15 January 1936	Birmingham City 0 Barnsley 2 FA Cup Third Round Replay

17	15 February 1936	Barnsley 2 Stoke City 1
		FA Cup Fifth Round
18	8 April 1939	Barnsley 2 Wrexham 1
		Football League Third Division North
19	10 January 1946	Barnsley 3 Newcastle United 0
		FA Cup Third Round 2nd Leg
20	11 January 1947	Huddersfield Town 3 Barnsley 4
		FA Cup Third Round
21	9 September 1950	Barnsley 6 Luton Town 1
		Football League Second Division
22	4 November 1950	Barnsley 7 Queens Park Rangers 0
		Football League Second Division
23	16 February 1952	Barnsley 5 Sheffield Wednesday 4
		Football League Second Division
24	10 January 1953	Barnsley 4 Brighton & Hove Albion 3
		FA Cup Third Round
25	3 May 1955	Barnsley 2 Rochdale 0
		Football League Division Three North
26	26 January 1957	Cardiff City 0 Barnsley 1
		FA Cup Fourth Round
27	4 September 1957	Barnsley 5 Ipswich Town 1
		Football League Second Division
28	6 February 1961	Barnsley 1 Huddersfield Town 0
		FA Cup Fourth Round Replay
29	18 February 1961	Barnsley 1 Luton Town 0
		FA Cup Fifth Round
30	8 March 1961	Barnsley 1 Leicester City 2
		FA Cup Sixth Round Replay
31	6 January 1964	Barnsley 3 Scunthorpe United 2
		FA Cup Third Round Replay
32	4 May 1968	Chester 1 Barnsley 1
		Football League Fourth Division
33	8 May 1979	Barnsley 2 Grimsby Town 1
		Football League Fourth Division
34	3 November 1979	Sheffield Wednesday 0 Barnsley 2
		Football League Third Division
35	28 April 1981	Barnsley 1 Rotherham United 0
		Football League Third Division
36	10 November 1981	Barnsley 4 Brighton & Hove Albion 1
		Football League Cup Third Round
37	2 December 1981	Barnsley 1 Manchester City 0
		Football League Cup Fourth Round

38	12 January 1982	Liverpool 0 Barnsley 0
		Football League Cup Quarter Final
39	2 October 1982	Barnsley 4 Fulham 3
		Football League Second Division
40	9 November 1982	Sheffield United 1 Barnsley 3
		Football League Cup Third Round
41	6 October 1987	West Ham United 2 Barnsley 5
		Football League Cup Second Round 2nd Leg
42	26 April 1997	Barnsley 2 Bradford City 0
		Football League Division One
43	9 August 1997	Barnsley 1 West Ham United 2
		Premier League
44	22 November 1997	Liverpool 0 Barnsley 1
		Premier League
45	4 February 1998	Barnsley 3 Tottenham Hotspur 1
		FA Cup Fourth Round Replay
46	25 February 1998	Barnsley 3 Manchester United 2
		FA Cup Fifth Round Replay
47	27 November 1998	Barnsley 7 Huddersfield Town 1
		Football League Division One
48	17 May 2000	Birmingham City 0 Barnsley 4
		Football League Division One Play-off Semi-Final 1st Leg
49	29 May 2000	Barnsley 2 Ipswich Town 4
		Football League Division One Play off Final
50	15 May 2006	Huddersfield Town 1 Barnsley 3
		Play-off Semi-Final 2nd Leg
51	27 May 2006	Barnsley 2 Swansea City 2
		Football League One Play-off Final (Barnsley won 4-3 on penalties)
52	16 February 2008	Liverpool 1 Barnsley 2
		FA Cup Fifth Round
53	9 March 2008	Barnsley 1 Chelsea 0
		FA Cup Sixth Round
54	6 April 2008	Barnsley 0 Cardiff City 1
		FA Cup Semi-Final

Arthur Kaye was one of Barnsley's best-ever wingers. Brian Elliott

1

Barnsley St Peter's v Liverpool

2 February 1895

F A Cup First Round
Oakwell, Barnsley
Attendance: 5,000 Receipts: £140

Barnsley St Peter's 1 Liverpool 2
Cutts   McVean, Ross

1894/95 was the last season that the Saints (Barnsley St Peter's) played in the Sheffield Challenge and the Wharncliffe Charity Cup competition before joining the Midland League in 1895/96.

For them to reach the 1st round of the FA Cup proper was a remarkable achievement. Along the way they beat Grantham Rovers 3–1, Leeds 8–0, Mexborough 1–0 (in a replay after a 1–1 draw), and finally Worksop Town 3–1.

The game against Liverpool created much excitement in the town and the attendance was an Oakwell record. On the Thursday before the game, the ground was covered in eight inches of snow. However, local men were engaged to prepare the pitch and on the Saturday the surface still had occasional patches of frozen snow, whilst the thaw which set in on the Friday had softened other areas.

St Peter's had to make several changes to their regular line-up. Right-winger Tom Smith was injured and Cutts took his place, Thompson moved to inside left and Vost took over at centre forward.

Alec Black won the toss for the Saints and opted to kick downhill. In the opening stages the visitors attack was on top, but Tom Nixon defended stoutly and with the help of Keech and Black kept them safely at bay. The first free kick fell to the Saints and a corner was conceded, but was cleared to safety. The visitors then gained possession, and after a good run, Ross, having dodged Nixon, had the goal at his mercy, but pulled his shot wide. The Saints tried to make headway, and a fruitless corner followed. Partridge had an opening, but Liverpool custodian McQueen saved and J McLean gave away a corner to prevent Bairstow from scoring. Drummond raced away giving Hannah a opening, but he failed miserably, then a Liverpool forward broke away in brilliant fashion, and goalkeeper Greaves effected a good save from Bradshaw.

The Barnsley St Peter's team of 1894/95 which played Liverpool in the FA Cup. Three of Barnsley's most notable players in their early days were Joseph Greaves, Tom Nixon and Alec Black. Pictured on the back row, Greaves [3rd from left] was the goalkeeper, signed from Sheffield Wednesday in 1893. He played 132 league and cup matches in 11 seasons. Next in line, Tom Nixon, was a full-back from Wombwell, the only player to appear in the the club's first season (1887) and the Reds' first game in the Football League against Lincoln City on 1 September 1898. He made 57 league and cup appearances. Alec Black was a wing-half who arrived at Oakwell from Edinburgh St Bernard's in October 1892. He also played for Glasgow Rangers and made 15 league and cup appearances for Barnsley, from 1892-99. D Wood

Directly afterwards the visitors broke away and McVean shot a lucky goal after 35 minutes play, the ball slowly passing over Greaves' foot in his attempt to kick the ball out. The play in the remaining 10 minutes was all in favour of Liverpool, whose forwards showed their skill and tactics to marked advantage.

Half-time: Barnsley St Peter's 0 Liverpool 1

When the contest was renewed McVean broke away and just shot wide, Greaves made an excellent save to deny the Merseysiders and Keech later headed away. Partridge then sped away and centred well, but Cutts missed the chance, and again he was at fault with an opportunity given to him by Black. Vost gave McQueen the hardest shot of the day, but he kept it out, though it cost a corner, but nothing further resulted. Liverpool were still in command and Ross after dodging Nixon left the ball for McVean, but he made a miserable attempt. St Peter's then broke away and Cutts equalised, with only 10 minutes left to play amid loud cheering.

Full Time: Barnsley St Peter's 1 Liverpool 1

Extra Time

The Barnsley officials were averse to restarting and lodged a verbal objection.

After a few minutes breathing time the referee decided to play half an hour of extra time.

The visitors at once worked hard, but were driven back. Vost had a good run and Hey sent in a couple of well directed shots which McQueen only just saved. Thompson then had a lovely chance, but lifted the ball over the crossbar. The visitors' defence were under pressure, but the Saints' attack was indifferent and the first quarter closed with the score still 1–1.

On the restart the visitors' forwards were exceedingly threatening, Drummond and Ross worked hard but could not get through. Hannah surged through the home defence with the ball at his toes, but Greaves dashed from goal to take the ball from him. Drummond then centred nicely and after one or two efforts, Ross scored the deciding goal with a weak shot which should have been cleared. Soon afterwards the final whistle blew with the score as follows:

Result: Barnsley St Peter's 1 Liverpool 2

Barnsley St Peter's: Greaves, Coupe and Nixon, Keech, Hey and Black, Cutts, Bairstow, Vost, Thompson and Partridge.
Liverpool: McQueen, Curran and D McLean, McCartney, McQue and J McLean, McVean, Ross, Bradshaw, Hannah and Drummond.

Referee: Mr M T Roberts (Derby). Linesmen: Messrs J Lowles and G Hickin

Protest by St Peter's

After the match, the officials of St Peter's lodged a protest with the referee against the win, under rule 17, which provides that extra time shall only be played when both teams mutually consent. It is contended in support of the protest that a verbal protest was made to the referee before the extra time was commenced, and therefore under the rule, the referee had no power to make extra time compulsory. The matter will come before the English Association and, if it is upheld, the match will have to be replayed at Liverpool.

Indeed the match was replayed at Liverpool nine days later, on 11 February, Liverpool winning 4-0. The attendance was approximately 4,000.

Season 1894/95: Sheffield Challenge Cup Competition

P	W	L	D	F	A
28	17	8	3	67	43

Wharncliffe Charity Cup Competition

P	W	L	D	F	A
10	4	5	1	19	21

Top scorer in the season: J Bairstow (15)

2

Lincoln City v Barnsley

1 September 1898

Football League Division Two
Sincil Bank, Lincoln
Attendance: 2,500

Lincoln City 1 Barnsley 0
Robertson

With the advent of September 1898, Barnsley Football Club embarked upon an entirely new era. From the Sheffield League, the club worked its way through the Sheffield competitions, then the Midland League, to finally secure a place in the prestigious Football League Division Two.

Surprisingly, the club's first ever game was scheduled for a Thursday afternoon in the city of Lincoln, against a team that had been members since 1892/93.

Barnsley had the advantage in the earliest exchanges, and a good return by Nixon was well utilised by the forwards, Lees putting in a fine shot, which Sharman saved. It is worthy of note that this was the first shot in the game, and that neither goalkeeper handled for a long time after that, and then it was Sharman who did. A series of throws took the visitors well into foreign country, but a free-kick drove them back, and Pugh, a former Irish international, and a brilliant right wing player was the most dangerous player on the Lincoln side, using his speed and trickery to good effect, and Porteous had his work cut out to stop him.

Murray in particular was playing a grand game for Barnsley, but try as they could, and they did try, they could not get past the sturdy home defence, maintained by the sturdy backs, McMillan and Gibson. As half-time drew near it became evident that there would be precious little scoring during the game. In half an hour, only one goalkeeper had been tested once, and the play had been very open. There were times when Barnsley had to defend grimly, but in such cases Tom Nixon's clean kicking and John McCartney's tackling kept all-comers at bay. The old Barnsley back was playing a grand game. In fact it is questionable if he ever played much better, and his play was the subject of admiration on all sides. It would be hard to imagine better play than that put in by Lees, Murray and McCullough, with occasional dashes by Davis and McGhee, the latter got in several fine centres and with one especially he had cruel luck. He centred straight across the goal, and McMillan had to kick the ball into touch, a corner kick ensuing. A few minutes later a grand run by Davis ended with a shot which only just went wide of the goal. When the referee blew his whistle for half-time, no goals had been scored, but Barnsley had much the better of the game so far.

Half-time: Lincoln City 0 Barnsley 0

Barnsley keeper Fawcett had not handled the ball at all in the first half, and Burleigh and Porteous were the better of the halves, whilst no fault could be found with the forwards. For the first thirty minutes or so in the second-half, the play was even. In the early part of the half, Barnsley pressed heavily, and twice Sharman was called upon, once from King and once from Porteous. But then a sudden change came over the scene, and Lincoln made all the running. Pugh began the attack with a really fine run on the right wing, his twenty yard shot going well wide. A minute later, Fawcett ran out a shot from the left wing, but missed the ball, which dropped over his head in front of an open goal, Porteous rushed up and kicked away in the nick of time, when a goal appeared a dead certainty. Following this, Lincoln urged on by a crowd of about 2,500 strong,

This photograph is believed to be the Barnsley team taken on Lincoln Town Hall steps from their first ever league match, on 1 September 1898.

Harry Davis. A native of Wombwell, Harry was the first player from the club to play for England (whilst with Sheffield Wednesday) in 1903, gaining three caps. At Oakwell the brilliant outside right scored 25 goals in 56 appearances, before moving to Hillsborough for £175 (plus William Simmons from Wednesday and a game at Barnsley, with the Reds taking the gate receipts).

pressed very heavily indeed, whilst on the other hand, Barnsley seemed to fall to pieces. Eventually the goal came, Robertson the centre forward put in a high shot which Fawcett, with a crowd of men around him, only partially cleared, and Robertson rushing up, planted the ball safely in the goal. This was after about 75 minutes play, and for the next five minutes Lincoln pressed heavily. During this period Nixon and Porteous conducted themselves admirably, especially Nixon. Porteous had all his work cut out again with Pugh, but did some good work in that direction, and Nixon kicked very finally, breaking up dangerous raids time after time in a manner which called forth unstinted applause. With about five minutes left Barnsley brightened up considerably, and play was transferred to the other end, it being very evident that Lincoln had not yet by any means won. Nixon from a free kick landed the ball well up, and shots from Burleigh and Murray were cleared by Sharman in fine style, the effort from centre forward Murray being a beauty. Up to the finish Barnsley continued to fight back hard, but they were unable to score, and time arrived with Lincoln City for once at the head of the table. Taking the game as a whole it had been a remarkably keen contest. At no point was the issue a certainty, and tributes to Barnsley's performance were given by the Lincoln directors.

All the team worked hard and the forwards, led by Murray, made a fine contribution. Burleigh and Porteous were the pick of the half-back line and at full-back, McCartney and Nixon were two good men, Nixon being by far and away the best player for the visitors.

In this first season, Barnsley finished Eleventh out of 18 teams, a creditable performance and one which silenced all the pre-season pessimists.

Result: Lincoln City 1 Barnsley 0

Lincoln City: Sharman, McMillan and Gibson, Smith, Bannister and Morris, Pugh, Henderson, Robertson, Fern and Clarke.
Barnsley: Fawcett, McCartney and Nixon, Burleigh, King and Porteous, Davis, Lees, Murray, McCullough and McGhee.

Season: 1898/99

P	W	L	D	F	A	Pts
34	12	15	7	52	56	31

Division: Two
Position: Eleventh
Secretary: Arthur Fairclough
Top Scorer: Harry Davis (15)

3

Barnsley v Blackpool

20 January 1910

FA Cup First Round Replay
Oakwell, Barnsley
Attendance: 13,939 Receipts: £438

Barnsley 6 Blackpool 0
Lillycrop (2),
Tufnell (2),
Gadsby, Boyle (pen)

Barnsley were unchanged from Saturday's 1–1 draw at Bloomfield Road, but the seasiders were forced into two changes, skipper Cox and Golding missing through injuries, sustained in the first match.

Both teams were locked together in the middle of the Second Division and a keenly fought contest was expected. Barnsley had the better of the early exchanges, and the visitors suffered a set-back after fifteen minutes' play when inside right Miller had to be carried off the pitch. He was accidentally kicked on the jaw, and his face was so badly cut, that he took no further part in the proceedings.

Barnsley's first goal came as a result of a penalty, Blackpool left back Whittingham handled a pass from Boyle, intended for Lillycrop. Boyle himself took the kick, driving the ball into the roof of the net, despite a great effort from Blackpool goalkeeper Fiske, who could only get his fingertips to the ball. Barnsley were now much more menacing and two minutes later, Bartrop had the ball in the net, but the goal was disallowed for a breach of the off-side rule by Tufnell. A brilliant shot from Bartrop was dealt with in splendid style by Fiske, but soon after he was beaten by Gadsby after a brilliant dribble between Lillycrop and himself, the centre forward making a magnificent opening for him.

Just on the interval, Barnsley registered a third goal, Forman raced down the left and whipped over a splendid centre, which enabled Lillycrop to place a clever header wide of the goalkeeper and into the corner of the goal.

Half-time: Barnsley 3 Blackpool 0

Lillycrop and particularly Boyle had been outstanding for Barnsley in the first

Ernest Gadsby, the scorer of Barnsley's second goal. He played only two seasons at Oakwell, scoring 16 goals in 53 appearances before moving to Bristol City in December 1910. He came from New Whittington, Chesterfield.

half. Short passing was difficult as the surface was a veritable sea of glue and Boyle's clever use of chipping the ball over the heads of the Blackpool defenders was paying rich dividends.

In the early part of the second half, Barnsley goalkeeper Mearns had his second shot to deal with, a long one from the visitors' outside left Dawson, and it was followed directly afterwards by the Reds' fourth goal. Lillycrop controlled another fine centre from Forman and placed the ball beautifully past Fiske. Then Tufnell was almost through, a fine shot compelling a corner. Forman then fired in a terrific shot, which hit one of the numerous Blackpool players swarming around Fiske. The Blackpool goalkeeper was again keeping splendidly, but he had not the slightest chance with Tufnell's hard hit shot which brought with it the fifth goal. Shortly afterwards, Forman banged in a smashing shot which Fiske saved, but the ball ran loose to Tufnell who shot goal number six.

Fiske in the Blackpool goal was the man of his side, and he was blameless for the shots which beat him. Mearns in the Barnsley goal is never again likely to have so quiet a time in a cup-tie. The excellent Glendenning, Boyle and Utley did everything required to combat a feeble Blackpool attack, whilst Lillycrop, Gadsby and Forman were outstanding for the Reds. The Blackpool full-backs and half-backs were no match for the speedy home forwards.

Result: Barnsley 6 Blackpool 0

Barnsley: Mearns, Downs and Ness, Glendenning, Boyle and Utley, Bartrop, Gadsby, Lillycrop, Tufnell and Forman.
Blackpool: Fiske, Gladwin and Whittingham, Threlfall, Connor and Clarke, J S Hoard, Miller, Beare, Wolstenholme and Dawson.

Referee: Mr J Baker

Note

The 6–0 victory was, and still is a record score for the Reds in an F A Cup match, and earned them a second round tie at Bristol Rovers. However, with Bristol City also being drawn at home, Rovers, for a consideration, transferred the match to Oakwell.

Season 1909/10

P	W	L	D	F	A	Pts
38	16	15	7	62	59	39

Division: Two
Position: Ninth
Manager: Arthur Fairclough
Top Scorer: George Lillycrop (23) - The first player to score over 20 goals in a season for the Reds.

4

Barnsley v Queens Park Rangers

5 March 1910

FA Cup Fourth Round
Oakwell, Barnsley
Attendance: 23,574 Receipts: £780

Barnsley 1 Queens Park Rangers 0
Bartrop

The attendance would have been much larger if accommodation had been available, but it was still Barnsley's biggest gate, and the first time that a crowd of over 20,000 had been locked in Oakwell. Though no exact figures were made available, it was estimated that many thousands were turned away at the gates, but 400 or so Rangers' fans managed to gain admission to watch their team, who incidently wore green and white hooped shirts and white shorts.

It was the first time that the two teams had met, Rangers being in the Southern League, and both teams were at near full strength. The ground was in perfect condition, and not a breath of air troubled the serenity of a magnificent spring day. The Rangers did all the attacking in the first fifteen minutes, when the strength of the Reds' defence was tested to its fullest extent. The forwards and the half-backs seemed to be almost overawed by the tremendous importance of the occasion. Neither Glendenning nor Utley showed at all well during this period, and Glendenning, though he improved much as soon as the novelty had worn off, was always apt to wander.

As the game wore on Barnsley began to improve, with Boyle being the instigator of it all and he shot for goal at every available opportunity. Occasionally the Rangers got into the Reds quarters, and one piece of footwork between Steer, Travers and McNaught was brilliantly executed. Ness, however, came to the rescue, and it was from his return that Gadsby was able to give Bartrop the glorious pass which led to the old Worksop player scoring a wonderful goal. For once Wake had left the Barnsley wing man free, and passing Fidler, Bartrop shot from a position only a few yards from the corner flag. Shaw tried to get at the ball, but missed it, and coming forward, he threw both Tufnell and Lillycrop, who were waiting to head the ball, quite off. It was well he did, for, coming down with perfect direction, the ball struck high up the upright, and glanced into the net. A mighty cheer greeted this success, and Bartrop was

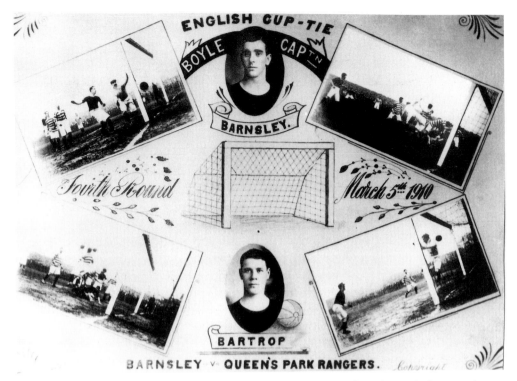

ENGLISH CUP-TIE

BOYLE CAP^{TN}

BARNSLEY.

Fourth Round

March 5th 1910

BARTROP

BARNSLEY v QUEEN'S PARK RANGERS. *Copyright*

Wilf Bartrop scored the only goal which put the Reds into their first FA Cup semi-final. A native of Worksop, he played outside-right and made 159 appearances, scoring 17 goals in six seasons at Oakwell before moving to Liverpool in March 1914.

overwhelmed with congratulations. The game quickly restarted, and for the remaining twenty minutes of the first half, the Rangers had a tremendous task before them. The best football of the whole game was seen during this period. Only a magnificent defence kept out the Barnsley forwards who were absolutely at their best during this period.

The importance of the occasion had not the slightest effect upon Boyle, however, and he was very largely responsible for the heaviness of the pressure which the Reds exerted in the closing stages of the half.

Half-time: Barnsley 1 Queens Park Rangers 0

At the opening of the second half Barnsley went away with great energy, and Bartrop was sadly at fault after a lovely centre by Forman which left him with an open goal. But Bartrop was not the only one who missed openings. In turn, Gadsby, Tufnell and Forman failed to improve upon positions which, on other occasions, would have been almost certain to produce goals. Towards the end the game became scrappy and, less than five minutes from the finish, Steer was heavily charged by Downs, having to be carried off the field injured, which turned out to be a fractured rib.

Boyle had played a tremendous game, he was quite the man of the match, some of his work being that of a football genius. Steer could do absolutely nothing with him, and time and time again Boyle left both Steer and Hartwell almost standing still, whilst he made chances for his forwards which they were unable to take up. Downs also played a great game. Mearns kept a fine goal, and Bartrop was the best forward, though nobody could have worked harder than Lillycrop did. But, above all, Boyle was the shining light.

Like Barnsley, the Rangers were strongest in defence, and it would be difficult to differentiate between the play of Fidler and McDonald. Travers was the best forward and Hartwell played a vigorous game at centre-half.

Making all allowances for the occasion, and giving every credit to the Rangers for a stubborn game, one is compelled to the impression that Barnsley are not playing as well as they did a month ago. All this success, in both league and cup tie football, has been got by twelve players. There have been few team changes since September and with this in mind, Barnsley's position amongst the semi-finals stands as an outstanding achievement - one which the supporters will look forward to in earnest.

Result: Barnsley 1 Queens Park Rangers 0

Barnsley: Mearns, Downs and Ness, Glendenning, Boyle and Utley, Bartrop, Gadsby, Lillycrop, Tufnell and Forman.
Queens Park Rangers: Shaw, McDonald and Fidler, Mitchell, Hartwell and Wake, McNaught, Travers, W Steer, Whyman and Barnes.

Referee: Mr F Heath (Birmingham)

5

Barnsley v Everton

31 March 1910

FA Cup Semi-Final Replay
Old Trafford, Manchester
Attendance: 55,000

Barnsley 3 Everton 0
Gadsby, Forman, Tufnell

Barnsley, to the great delight of their many followers, qualified for the final of the FA Cup by achieving a magnificent victory over First Division Everton at the second time of asking. When the clubs met at Leeds in the first game, it was felt

Tommy Boyle (left) at the toss with Everton's skipper John Sharp, who was a dual England international at football and cricket. Boyle was one of the Reds best ever defenders and notched 19 goals (mostly penalties) in 178 games in a career that stretched from 1906 to 1911 before he moved to Burnley for a fee of £1,250.

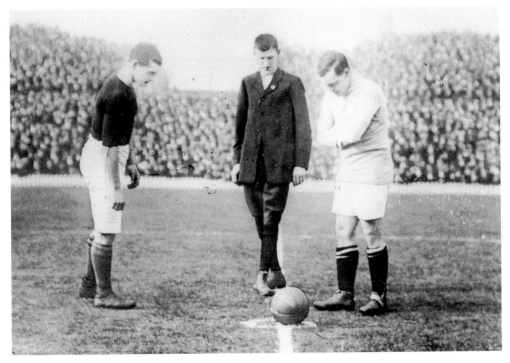

by many that a 0–0 draw was the best that the Reds could achieve. But those who entertained such an opinion proved to be quite out in their reckoning.

If in the first game Barnsley rose to the occasion in gallant style, they went one better in the replay, and beat their redoubtable opponents on their merits. The margin of three goals to nil may be regarded as extraordinary, but no one can deny that Barnsley deserved their remarkable triumph. At no time during a great game did they look like being on the losing side, and if Everton had hard luck in having two players injured and playing with ten men for the greater part of the game, the winning team, were, always superior to their opponents and won simply through superior pace and stamina.

The contest created even more interest than the previous one, and 55,000 people were attracted to the commodious enclosure at Old Trafford. Both clubs were again supported by huge bands of supporters and the majority of the crowd were again of the opinion that the larger playing area would favour the first division team. However, the speed of the Reds' wingers told its tale, and by the finish Everton were entirely run off their feet.

The spacious ground was filled long before the start, and such a scene as the great amphitheatre presented might have overawed men made of less sterner stuff than the South Yorkshire combination, but they entered the fray as if was an every week occurrence. The playing pitch was like a billiard table, and there was not a single bare patch on the newly turfed ground.

Tommy Boyle won the toss and Everton started against the wind, the Reds having to clear a troublesome right wing move involving Sharp and Young. Everton were then penalised for offside, and then Downs easily robbed Barlow and White who were making headway. Barnsley were then awarded a free-kick, which Forman placed into the Everton penalty area, but Boyle shot wide from an awkward position. Heading away a shot from Forman, Clifford gave his forwards possession, but Glendenning stopped the attack, and the Barnsley right half set up Bartrop for a first time shot which Scott saved. A capital run by Bartrop, Lillycrop, and Forman saw the Reds assume the aggressive but Harris stopped them. Forman was soon busy again when Lillycrop passed to him, but he could do no better than force a corner. From the flag kick Utley headed wide. But it was a very near thing and deserved the applause that greeted the attempt.

Shortly after Everton centre half Taylor injured his thorax and he took no further part in the game. This unfortunate accident occurred after only twelve minutes play and the Toffeemen had to re-arrange their team. Makepeace went to centre half, White to left half with Sharp on his own on the right wing. However, Barnsley were playing with even greater confidence than in the first game, and at no period were to lose their grip on the game.

Play went from end to end, Ness clearing for the Reds and Clifford doing likewise for the Lancastrians. Scott saved from Gadsby, and also cleared a header from the same player. Forman also tested him, but the custodians task was easy. Utley pulled up Sharp at a critical moment and Bartrop missed the upright with a fine shot.

Barnsley came again, and Harris handled in the penalty area. It was not a glaring offence, and the referee consulted the linesman before awarding a penalty. Boyle took the kick, amid intense excitement, but shot wide, a groan from the Barnsley contingent accompanying the effort. The Reds made another effort to get through, but Forman was robbed and Everton went downfield and with Young looking dangerous, Ness brought him down. The referee immediately awarded a spot kick, but Mearns diving to his right brought off a magnificent save from Sharp, and the crowd cheered wildly. The Barnsley players almost fell on Mearns, but the keeper waved them away in the coolest fashion. There was only four minutes to go to the interval and Young and Freeman made a strenuous effort to get through, but finished weakly, Downs easily punting the ball upfield.

Half-time: Barnsley 0 Everton 0

Although only playing with ten men, Everton forced the game in the second half, and for some minutes kept play in the Barnsley territory. Sharp had a grand opportunity to score, but hesitated before an open goal, and when he did shoot, the ball was charged down by Downs. Everton came again in promising style, but Barlow was adjudged offside. Play was very exciting and favoured Everton, but their forwards were very slow when near the Barnsley goal. When the Oakwell men did get to the other end, Boyle shot high over the bar. Then came a combined rush on the part of the Barnsley forwards, which had a remarkable effect on the game. Boyle sent to Forman, who was well placed, and the left-winger sprinted down the line before driving the ball across the goalmouth. Goalkeeper Scott grabbed at it, but lost possession. Lillycrop and Gadsby were close on him, however, the ball eventually fell to Gadsby who shot it into the net amid a great display of enthusiasm by the Barnsley supporters. It was a good goal, but in the melee Scott was injured. He had to receive medical aid, his fingers and wrist being damaged. He did not leave the field, but Maconnachie temporarily took his place.

Still, Everton played as if they were out to win, and they had several chances, but were unable to take them. Freeman in particular was led by his collegues admirably, but through dallying with the ball Everton forwards were frequently robbed in the easiest of fashions. One shot, however, by Freeman was near the mark, but Mearns cleared cleverly and on another occasion the Barnsley custodian ran out and took the ball from Freeman's toe when the latter had the backs beaten.

Scott soon resumed, and the Lancastrians pressed heavily, the play of the Barnsley team falling away. Young went full tilt for the Barnsley goal, and

Mearns ran out and missed the leather altogether. Fortunately the sphere went on the wrong side of the upright. Sharp put in a shot that went too high, and Downs got the better of Young when the Evertonian was in a splendid position. Mearns also cleared grandly from a corner, and Ness headed away in the nick of time.

A sudden rush by the Barnsley forwards enabled Lillycrop to get through and he passed to Gadsby who was offside, but he still netted the ball. Both Gadsby and Glendenning sustained slight injuries, and Downs twice cleared his lines, both times the leather finishing out of the ground. As the game neared the end Barnsley took full command. First Forman got away and then Bartrop followed suit and with ten minutes to go the ten men of Everton began to wilt. They could not hold the Barnsley attack in which Forman played a distinguished part. The Barnsley players swung the ball about in winning fashion and with six minutes to play, Lillycrop led an attack on the Everton goal, passing to Bartrop who centred well, Forman received possession, and promptly dispatched a shot well out of Scott's reach for goal number two. The Reds came again with a swift movement but Gadsby missed easily when at close quarters. The Everton defence, however, could not keep the Barnsley forwards back and Gadsby swung

Tom Forman scoring the vital second goal in the 3-0 win. Tom was a Nottinghamshire lad, signed from Sutton Town in 1907 and scored 18 goals in 138 appearances before moving to Tottenham Hotspur in November 1911.

32

over yet another centre and Tufnell headed it out of Scott's reach and into the net for number three and sent the Oakwell men into their first ever FA Cup final.

The victorious team were strong from back to front. Mearns, apart from his penalty save, had little to do in goal, but did it perfectly. Downs and Ness were both powerful and safe at full-back and very skilful and resolute in their tackling. The wing halves, Glendenning, Boyle and Utley smothered the Everton forwards, with Utley in particular outstanding. In attack, Bartrop, Gadsby and Tufnell played their part. Lillycrop led the line with intelligence, always bringing his flankmen into action and Forman was quite the best forward on either side.

Result: Barnsley 3 Everton 0

Barnsley: Mearns, Downs and Ness, Glendenning, Boyle and Utley, Bartrop, Gadsby, Lillycrop, Tufnell and Forman.
Everton: Scott, Macconachie and Clifford, Makepeace, Taylor and Harris, Barlow, Young, Freeman, White and Sharp.

Referee: Mr H S Bartlett (Gateshead)
Linesmen: Messrs A Adams (Nottingham) and J Dickerson (Herts)

Barnsley v Newcastle United

23 April 1910

FA Cup Final
Crystal Palace, London.
Attendance: 77,747

Barnsley 1 Newcastle United 1
Tufnell   Rutherford

Barnsley were unchanged from their semi-final victory over Everton, with Newcastle introducing Shepherd at centre forward in place of Stewart.

The Reds immediately made inroads down the left when Boyle swept it out to Forman who slipped it past full-back McCracken, but unfortunately saw the ball roll out of play for a goal kick.

Shepherd then tried a shot, which Mearns handled well, but when Downs misjudged a header, it seemed that Higgins would get through, but fortunately Ness spotted the danger and managed to get his foot to the ball and punt it clear.

Fred Mearns, the Barnsley goalkeeper, saving from a Newcastle forward during the 1910 FA Cup Final at Crystal Palace. *Illustrated London News*

The Barnsley defence at this time was playing remarkably well, that slip of Downs being an exception, and Boyle and Utley seemed well on top of their game.

Lillycrop then got the Reds moving towards the Geordies' goal and centre half Low deliberately pushed him in the back to give Barnsley their first free kick. Boyle took the kick, and placed to Glendenning, who almost lost the ball, but recovered it in time to dodge a couple of opponents in his own sweet way. He finished his part of the business by transferring to Gadsby, who took three steps forward, shouldered off Whitsun with a perfect heave, and tipped the ball to Bartrop. So far the movement had been ideal, but the outside right, instead of crossing, tried a shot which went wide. Then Barnsley attacked again, and Forman had a chance, but McCracken was too good for him.

Then referee Ibbotson twice made mistakes in letting Newcastle forwards go on when they were clearly offside. The Geordies' left-winger Wilson who up to now had not been in the game wandered into the centre and surprised Boyle, but Downs nipped in to clear. Veitch then got possession, made a brilliant dribble, but instead of feeding his forwards, he decided to try a shot on his own which hit the side netting. Howie a moment later had a great opportunity to get in a deadly centre but he dallied to such an extent that Utley was able to come back and concede a corner, from which the Barnsley goal had a narrow escape.

Just when it appeared that Newcastle were getting on top, Barnsley hit them with a surprise goal in the 38th minute which changed the whole complexion of the game. Though the Reds had challenged keeper Lawrence on two or three occasions, there had been nothing in their forward play to suggest that they were going to open the scoring. Downs began this movement by taking the ball from Wilson with consummate ease, and when he put the ball along the touchline

Bartrop gathered it but then hesitated. Gadsby, however, had summed up the situation and motioning his partner to take the inside berth where Whitsun was waiting, Gadsby put the ball past the Newcastle back but could not advance further because Whitsun obstructed him. However, the ball broke to Bartrop who taking the ball in his stride, put over a perfect centre which Lillycrop jumped over. Tufnell coolly collected the ball and placed it wide of Lawrence into the net. It was a well worked goal and brought much delight to the hearts of the Barnsley excursionists.

After this reverse Newcastle put more dash into their play, and from a beautiful centre by Wilson, Shepherd headed towards goal but Mearns was equal to the task.

Half-time: Barnsley 1 Newcastle United 0

Changing ends, Newcastle altered the arrangements of their forward line, Wilson and Higgins their left wing pair, changing places with each other. Play grew vigorous and was fairly even and there were several stoppages owing to players on both sides receiving hard knocks, Boyle and Bartrop on the Barnsley side especially suffering.

Barnsley continued to press and had recognised that Whitsun, the Newcastle left-back, was the weak link in defence and it soon became obvious that Bartrop was to be asked to do the damage. The winger stuck to his task well, but quite often his centres could never be turned to account simply because McCracken was playing the game of his life. The big Irishman was never at fault, clearing a wonderful amount of ground, and he never hesitated to put the Barnsley forwards off-side, although considering some of Mr Ibbotson's ideas on the offside rule, that was a rather risky thing to do. But McCracken's offside movements were made with such rare judgment that there was never any doubt about the correctness of his claim, and so many fine Barnsley movements were nipped in the bud. The Newcastle half-backs, however, were being run off their feet hereabouts, and Low was so much bothered that he had to take a summary means of stopping Boyle and Bartrop. The outside right was so badly damaged that he had to be attended to on the touchline, and his absence gave the Newcastle defence a rest. At this time Higgins and Wilson had changed places, and the new formation gave Downs a lot more trouble than he had received in the first half. He showed, however, that McCracken was not the only great back on view. Then Wilson got away and shot across goal, Shepherd rushed up and forced the ball into the net, but was clearly off-side.

The strain of keeping the lead was beginning to tell on the Barnsley rearguard but they were still defending well enough to see to it that Mearns had practically nothing to do. Glendenning was a very prominent figure at this point, and his tackling of Wilson and Higgins drew applause over and over again. Boyle then managed to get his forwards going and Forman managed to get past McCracken, and put in a centre which was headed by Lillycrop into Lawrence's hands.

With eight minutes to go and with the Reds looking by far the better side, the wife of the Barnsley Manager Mrs Fairclough removed the red ribbon from her umbrella to tie on the cup. However, within seconds of the act, disaster struck for the Reds. Taking a long pass from Veitch, Higgins on the extreme left wing got across a centre that was passing in front of goal, when outside right Rutherford rushed up and skilfully seized a golden opportunity to head past Mearns for the equaliser. However, most people in the ground believed that Rutherford was well offside and so unanimous was the appeal of the Barnsley defence that it was expected the referee would disallow the goal. However, Mr Ibbotson would have none of it, and bearing in mind his earlier interpretation of the offside rule, this should have come of no surprise to the Barnsley contingent. The last few minutes petered out without any further incidents and the stalemate meant a replay would be required at Goodison Park.

Result: Barnsley 1 Newcastle United 1

Barnsley: Mearns, Downs and Ness, Glendenning, Boyle and Utley, Bartrop, Gadsby, Lillycrop, Tufnell and Forman.
Newcastle United: Lawrence, McCracken and Whitsun, Veitch, Low and McWilliam, Rutherford, Howie, Shepherd, Higgins and Wilson.

Referee: Mr J T Ibbotson, (Derby)
Linesmen: Messrs T Kyle (Aylebury) and R Walker (Accrington)

The Replay

The crowd at Goodison Park was 65,000 and the gates were closed before the kick off. It was estimated by the police that there was at least 15,000 outside unable to gain admission. Over 20,000 travelled from Barnsley for the match, but unfortunately the Reds didn't play as well as they could, and at half-time the score sheet was blank.

However, after 51 minutes Higgins pushed the ball through for Shepherd to run and shoot past Mearns into the net. Bartrop missed a great chance to equalise and then Ness brought down Shepherd in the area. The same player picked himself up and planted the spot kick well out of the reach of Mearns and the cup was on its way to the North-East.

The supporters were naturally disappointed, but nevertheless there was a tremendous reception for the team when they returned home and the crowd packed the streets of Barnsley to give the team a hero's welcome.

The Reverend Preedy who had founded the club was still working in London, and recalled the origins of the club in his letter of congratulations to the Reds. Naturally he was proud that the team which might never have come into existence but for him should have achieved such a great distinction. An extract from his letter stated: 'The Pioneers of Soccer at St Peter's were a good bunch of young men. Our success was by no means instantaneous, rugger was the game up to then and the new style met with determined opposition. Everyone seemed to be against us, the people, the press, but we fought on. The team never bothered about gates, only goals.'

It could be said that Barnsley Football Club was on the map at last and there was no doubt that the performance of reaching an FA Cup Final had astonished the rest of the football world.

7

Barnsley v Bradford City

21 March 1912

FA Cup Fourth Round, 3rd Replay
Bramall Lane, Sheffield
Attendance: 38,264

Barnsley 3 Bradford City 2
Lillycrop (2)   Spiers, Devine
Travers

The match at Bramall Lane was the fourth time that the two teams had met, all of the previous three games being drawn 0–0. The third game at Elland Road, Leeds ended after eighty-five minutes due to the conditions and continuous rain and sleet would mean similar conditions for the teams at Bramall Lane.

Bradford City were the current Cup holders and were determined not to give up their trophy without a fight. Barnsley had to make one change from the Elland Road game, Jimmy Moore deputising for the injured Bert Leavey, who had broken his leg in the previous encounter.

G. TRAVERS

The game began at a frantic pace and after several near misses Barnsley took the lead after thirteen minutes, Travers taking a pass from Lillycrop, turning and in a single movement despatching a fierce low shot across goalkeeper Mellors and into the far corner of the net. Then from a centre by Bartrop, Lillycrop with a beautiful shot was within an ace of scoring again, and a little later he gave Travers another glorious chance to increase the Reds' lead, but unhampered and favourably placed, with plenty of time and plenty of room, the

George Travers, scorer of Barnsley's first goal, was signed from Leicester City in January 1911 and scored 25 goals in 101 league and cup games before joining Manchester United in February 1914.

George Lillycrop scored two of Barnsley's goals. He scored 104 goals in 233 games for Barnsley before being transferred to Bolton Wanderers in August 1913.

inside left lifted the ball over the bar. Bradford's left half McDonald was very unfortunate when he unleashed a fine shot which beat Cooper in the Barnsley goal but hit the angle of the goalposts, and shortly afterwards Thompson was equally unlucky in not equalising with a similar effort. However, on the balance of play, Barnsley deserved to go to half-time with a one goal lead.

Half-time: Barnsley 1 Bradford City 0

The second half followed a similar pattern to the first, but after 65 minutes, a well placed corner from Thompson enabled inside right Spears to head a splendid equaliser. City were now in the ascendancy and ten minutes later Devine, taking a pass from Logan on the right, tricked Downs and gave Cooper no chance with a fine shot to put the Cup holders ahead. Barnsley then seemed to lose their way somewhat, and for a time played like a beaten team. Eventually they awoke to a great effort, and with time running out and only five minutes left, Tufnell had a shot turned away by the goalkeeper for a corner. From Moore's kick, Lillycrop leapt to head a dramatic equalising goal and the crowd went wild with excitement and enthusiasm. The last couple of minutes were thrilling, as Lillycrop hit the Bradford bar and Thompson the Barnsley upright.

Full time: Barnsley 2 Bradford City 2

With the score two goals each extra time was played, and on the heavy ground the well trained teams kept up the pace wonderfully well. First one side and then the other attacked, and everyone was expecting yet another replay, when the game ended in a sensational fashion. In the last 30 seconds Barnsley made one last desperate burst. Bartrop drove the ball in and Mellors beat it out; Glendenning sent it across to Lillycrop, who hooked it into the net as Mellors, who had scarcely recovered from his previous save, vainly threw himself at it. Lillycrop at first seemed scarcely to know what had happened, but when he realised that he had scored a winning goal, he danced with delight until smothered by his joyous comrades. This was the last kick of the match, for before the ball could be placed in the centre circle, the referee's whistle sounded time. The Reds had beaten the Cup holders and were now in the semi-final of the FA Cup for the second time in three years.

In winning by the odd goal in five, Barnsley had their just deserts. To this extent they were the superior team. Equal to the Cup holders in defence, they were speedier in attack with centre forward George Lillycrop being the outstanding forward on view. He led the line with good judgment, passed well, shot well, was dashing and bold, and scored an equalising goal and finally a winning one. The experiment of playing Moore, a right-winger, in the position of outside left was an unqualified success, so much that Leavey was not missed. The win meant that the Reds would play Swindon Town in the semi-final at Crystal Palace.

Result: Barnsley 3 Bradford City 2

Barnsley: Cooper, Downs and Taylor, Glendenning, Bratley and Utley, Bartrop, Tufnell, Lillycrop, Travers and Moore.
Bradford City: Mellors, Campbell and Gane, Hampton, Torance and McDonald, Logan, Spiers, Walden, Devine and Thompson.

Referee: Mr A Adams (Nottingham)

Season 1911/12

P	W	L	D	F	A	PTS
38	15	11	12	45	42	42

Division: Two
Position: Sixth
Manager: Arthur Fairclough
Top Scorer: Harry Tufnell (11)

8

Barnsley v Swindon Town

3 April 1912

FA Cup Semi-Final Replay
Meadow Lane, Nottingham
Attendance: 18,000 Receipts: £1,058

Barnsley 1 Swindon Town 0
Bratley

For the second time in three years, Barnsley reached the FA Cup Final, by beating Swindon Town by the only goal of the game.

The first game at Stamford Bridge, Chelsea, four days earlier had been an epic encounter and a crowd of 48,057 had paid £2,985 5s 6d, the largest amount ever taken at a semi-final up to that time. In a bitterly fought game there were many stoppages and at the final whistle both teams were lucky to end with eleven men; but the 0–0 draw meant a second battle. The southern press gave Barnsley a lot of stick, saying that they had used unfair tactics, but on the foul count, Swindon had made more rash tackles than the Reds.

Swindon's key player, Harold Fleming did not make the second game, but Lillycrop and Glendenning, who had both been injured at Stamford Bridge, made the replay thanks to a couple of days rest at Matlock, where the Reds had refreshed themselves after Saturday's game.

On a firm pitch, the unchanged Reds had to contend with the sun in their faces in the first half, the conditions being much in Swindon's favour. In their changed strip of Oxford Blue, Barnsley had to contend with a stream of Swindon attacks, mainly through their left wing pair of Brown and Lamb. However, keeper Jack Cooper was as cool as a cucumber, but the men in front of him became overborne by excitement caused by the importance of the occasion and, for the first/ten minutes or so, Barnsley struggled to get out of their own half.

Eventually, Downs, Bratley and Utley got a grip of the situation and Moore began to get the better of Handley and Kay on the right side of the Swindon defence. From one of his many centres, Travers, the Reds' inside left, should have done better, but drove his shot wide of a gaping goal.

Bartrop on the Barnsley right flank was not seeing much of the ball and was consequently very quiet indeed. Lillycrop was distributing passes freely, but not lengthily, but was still working like a Trojan and one fine effort from him was

Goalkeeper Jack Cooper who saved a penalty to keep the Reds in the tie. He made 192 appearances between 1908 and 1918.

only inches too high. Handley the Swindon right half trying to intercept a cross from Bartrop nearly sliced the ball into his own net, as the Reds began to assert their authority.

When Swindon did get a move on, it was their right wing that progressed, and Jefferson beat both Utley and Taylor, and then centred. Burkinshaw ran up and appeared certain to score, but to the joy of the Yorkshiremen, sent his effort wide. That was a very narrow escape for the Reds and another chance came for Swindon but the former Rotherham player frittered it away. After that, Taylor, Bratley and Downs took full control and for a while Swindon were kept well out of range and there seemed little for the Reds to fear.

Moore and Bartrop started to get the measure of Walker and Kay the Swindon full-backs and this led to some very exciting incidents in the Swindon goalmouth. There was one particular thrilling period at this part of the game, which was when Moore tricked Kay and, dribbling in, sent the ball across the mouth of the goal, only a yard out. Lillycrop tried to force it in, but Skiller the Swindon keeper just reached it with his fingers. In another of these attacks, Moore struck the bar and Lillycrop just sent his shot over the bar. Once the ball was driven in with terrific speed by Tufnell, but it struck Walker's shoulder as he stood near the goal, and had he not been there, Skiller would have stood no earthly chance.

Swindon worked their way back into the game with some neat inter-passing and Lamb worked to within a few yards of Cooper, but Downs threw himself bodily at the ball and it shot into touch. During this period Barnsley had their narrowest escape of the match. In the 35th minute Jefferson, who appeared suspiciously offside and in a very dangerous position, got away from Utley, but the big Reds' wing half hauled him down and the referee awarded the Robins a penalty. Inside left Brown took the spot kick, but Cooper, diving to his right, fisted the ball away, much to the delight of the Barnsley contingent.

Half-time: Barnsley 0 Swindon Town 0

Swindon's failure to convert their spot kick cost them dearly, for the Reds redoubled their efforts and Skiller in the Swindon goal became a very busy man indeed. First Lillycrop, who gave some neat passes, tested Skiller and then both Travers and Moore were only just wide of the goal with further efforts. There was also shouts for a penalty when Moore was tripped in the penalty area, but the referee appealed to a linesman who seemed to be running away from the incident, and the combined opinions negated such a concession to the Oakwell men.

The succeeding play was all in Barnsley's favour. Lillycrop shot past the post and Kay just stopped Moore after a fine run by the latter. Moore then wasted another chance by dithering, not knowing whether to shoot or pass. Travers then lobbed a centre onto the crossbar, and Bartrop sped away to fire in a shot which appeared to be going inside the post, but Skiller dived to his right to turn the ball out for a corner. This was after 57 minutes and it signalled the goal that was to put the Reds in the final. Bartrop's flag kick was perfectly placed and centre half Phil Bratley ran through unchallenged to send a thumping header past Skiller and into the roof of the net.

After that, Moore, Bartrop and Travers all tried their luck, Moore and Bartrop only failing by inches to beat Skiller again. Burkinshaw swapped places with Wheatcroft, but to no avail, for the southern forwards could never get going, and it was 37 minutes of the second half before Jefferson managed to get in a shot for the Robins.

Barnsley's superior strength and determination was a demonstration of how

well they had been trained and Swindon were fortunate that in the last few minutes the Reds forwards wasted chance after chance to register a more comprehensive victory.

Barnsley shone in all departments, except that of shooting of course, for they should have won by at least three or four goals. Cooper in goal had not a great deal to do, yet there was tremendous force in the penalty kick he saved. Taylor played a splendid game at full-back, but he naturally did not take the eye quite so much as Downs, who not only defended in great style, but kicked with almost unfailing

Phil Bratley headed the winning goal in the 57th minute. Bratley made 124 appearances for Barnsley, between 1910 -14, scoring 8 goals.

accuracy. Downs indeed carried off the chief honours of the match, playing the finest game of the day.

The Barnsley halves covered themselves with glory: Glendenning was good, and Bratley and Utley were even better in tackling and placing the ball to their forwards. The pick of the front rank were the two wingmen, Bartrop and Moore. Bartrop only got his chances in the second half, but Moore was easily the best forward on view. Lillycrop did well, but was a distributor rather than an attacker. Both Tufnell and Travers were quick and smart, though Travers hung on to the ball too much. There were times when the combination of the front five was not what it should have been, but they made up for any shortcomings in this respect by the effort and energy they put into their play. It was this vigour which was answerable for disconcerting the Swindon team. On the whole the combination was vastly ahead of what was seen at Stamford Bridge in the first game.

Special mention must be made of the Barnsley fans; despite the absence of excursions, thousands poured out of the town to support their team. Several batches of men left the Barnsley district the day before the match, whilst scores of cyclists rode there, the fine weather being all in favour of this. A number of people went by train, but the greater portion went by road, dozens of motors, taxi cabs, charabangs, and even lorries being requisitioned to bring passengers from all over South Yorkshire.

Result: Barnsley 1 Swindon Town 0

Barnsley: Cooper, Downs and Taylor, Glendenning, Bratley and Utley, Bartrop, Tufnell, Lillycrop, Travers and Moore
Swindon Town: Skiller, Kay and Walker, Handley, Silto and Chambers, Jefferson, Burkinshaw, Wheatcroft, Brown and Lamb.

Referee: Mr H S Bartlett (Gateshead)
Linesmen: Messrs, L P Morrison and A H Oakley

9

Barnsley v West Bromwich Albion

24 April 1912

FA Cup Final Replay
Bramall Lane, Sheffield
Attendance: 38,555 Receipts: £2,645 9s

Barnsley 1 West Bromwich Albion 0
Tufnell

Both teams were unchanged from the first game at Crystal Palace four days earlier, Barnsley resting at Matlock, as they did for their semi-final replay against Swindon Town.

The Throstles (WBA) were first on the attack and Cooper had to deal with a long shot. Barnsley got away on the left but were penalised for offside, Travers being the culprit. Play was fast and furious, and Taylor twice stopped the Albion forwards. The Albion then had a free kick in the Barnsley quarters, but there was not the slightest danger to the Reds' citadel. Pearson then thwarted Utley, and Bartrop's wild effort went yards wide. Shearman tried a shot at the Barnsley

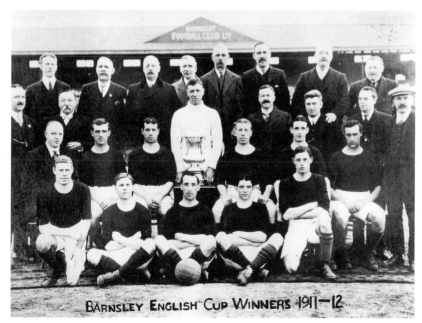

The team.
Back row (L-R): Glendenning, Downs, Cooper, Taylor (capt), Bradley, Utley.
Front row (L-R): Bartrop, Tufnell (goalscorer), Lillycrop, Travers, Moore.

goal, but that too went harmlessly by. Bartrop then beat Pennington to a through ball, but all the other Reds' forwards failed to reach his centre. Bartrop put in more good work, but Lillycrop headed his centre over the bar. Play continued to be fast and furious, Barnsley being more in the picture than the Throstles. Moore then lost possession, but shortly afterwards tested Pearson's goal with the best shot so far, the keeper holding on to the ball with much difficulty.

After an hour's play, Utley gave the left-winger a neat pass, and Moore shot in strongly. Yet again Pearson caught the ball, and cleared amid much excitement. Barnsley were on top at this stage, and Bartrop got in a shot which Pearson missed, and the ball fell in front of an unguarded goal. Travers and Moore went for the ball, but the latter missed with a fine effort. The Albion had a corner and a free kick near goal in quick succession, Cooper clearing easily from Wright, but play continued for a while in the Barnsley quarters. Then Travers broke away, but he finished with a weak shot. Pearson fisted out a shot from Glendenning, and when Albion broke into the Reds' half, Shearman had a chance to centre but put his effort behind for a goal kick.

Half-time: Barnsley 0 West Bromwich Albion 0

On the resumption Barnsley were quick off the mark, and Bartrop just managed to reach the ball on the touchline; he centred, but Pearson caught the ball and averted any danger. A corner followed to Barnsley, but nothing came of it. Bowser tested Cooper at the other end and the Throstles had two free kicks in the Reds' territory. Neither proved of any advantage to the Albion and the Yorkshire side attacked vigorously, but Bartrop was yards wide with his effort on the run. 'Barnsley' was the general cry and Lillycrop made a great effort to get through but then shot wide. Moore was injured and play was stopped for a while. After a period of midfield play, Albion forced a corner on the right. Downs got the ball away and a swift movement downfield saw Pearson save a low shot from Lillycrop. Moore then tricked three opponents, and finally shot yards the wrong side of the goal.

Barnsley were now pressing hard, but they did not test Pearson unduly. When Albion next attacked the Yorkshire citadel had a narrow escape. Jephcott got in a fine centre which was missed by two or three players, and when Bowser got the leather and shot, Cooper was up to the task which was a great relief to the Reds. Barnsley then made tracks to the other end, but were stopped on two occasions by Pennington. Bartrop then broke away and beat the Albion defence, but his centre was missed by Moore. Glendenning neatly robbed Shearman when the latter was making tracks for goal, and when Pailor handled a free kick it relieved the pressure. Albion were pressing at this point and Jephcott got clear away on the right, and Cooper had his work cut out to save his final shot. Minutes later the Albion swarmed around the Reds' goal and Cooper did well to

Harry Tufnell, Barnsley's FA Cup Final goalscoring hero. He was one of the Club's longest serving players prior to the First World War. He notched 70 goals in 239 games between 1909-1920.

tip a capital shot from Pailor over the bar. Nothing came of the corner kick, Taylor clearing with ease and a few seconds later the full time whistle blew.

Full time: Barnsley 0 West Bromwich Albion 0

Extra Time

The first quarter opened in midfield. Moore got in the first shot, but Pearson saved the sphere and threw it up-field. Pennington gave a corner to prevent Lillycrop getting through, and when play switched to the other end Cooper had to concede a corner to stop Shearman. The flag kick was got away, but Downs injured his leg in a collision. Cooper then made a mess of a centre by Shearman, but Bratley came to his rescue to save the situation. The same player shot in at the other end, but Pearson had no difficulty in getting the ball away. Travers skimmed the bar with a lightning shot and directly after Shearman got through but robbed in the danger zone. A corner fell to Barnsley, but the Throstles cleared and the interval arrived with no score.

On resuming, the Albion made a dash for the Barnsley goal, but Downs was in the way, and when Barnsley got going they were pulled up by Pennington. Bartrop made a weak effort, and West Brom gained a corner, but it was of no advantage. The Reds now invaded the Throstles' goal and Pearson only partially cleared a shot from Moore; and Bartrop shot in, but Cook was in the way, and when Bratley shot the leather it cannoned off the post. It was now all pressure from the Reds and how the Albion goal escaped is a mystery. The Midlanders responded with a corner, but the flag kick by Jephcott was useless. A second corner fell to the Albion, and Cooper cleverly saved two smart efforts. He fisted away the flag kick, and then cleared from Pailor. Glendenning then called upon Pearson at the other end and the custodian was equal to it.

With only two minutes to go it seemed another game would be required, when Glendenning received possession in midfield. He quickly spotted the Throstles' backs were well apart and put the ball between them. Tufnell was on to it in a flash and neither Cook or Pennington had the speed to catch him. Pearson advanced from his citadel, but Tufnell steadied himself and slotted the leather past the custodian just inside the right hand post, to give the Reds the lead.

The spectators rushed on to the field and Tufnell was overwhelmed by players and spectators alike. The last two minutes went by and the game ended amid scenes of terrific excitement. When the final whistle went, Pennington, the Albion skipper and an England international rushed across to Taylor, his Barnsley counterpart, and warmly shook his hand.

Result: Barnsley 1 West Bromwich Albion 0

Barnsley: Cooper, Downs and Taylor, Glendenning, Bratley and Utley, Bartrop, Tufnell, Lillycrop, Travers and Moore.
West Bromwich Albion: Pearson, Cook and Pennington, Baddeley, Buck and McNeal, Jephcott, Wright, Pailor, Bowser and Shearman.

Referee: Mr J R Schumacher (London)
Linesmen: Messrs M Billson (Leicester) and W F Hiscock (Kent)

Comments

The team had done the town of Barnsley proud. In twelve FA Cup games, they had conceded only three goals, a record which stood right up to 1976, when Fulham equalled it when they too reached the final. The Reds' team was made up of ten Englishmen, and one Scotsman, Taylor the captain. Cooper and Bartrop came from Nottinghamshire, Downs, Glendenning, Lillycrop and Moore from the North East, Travers from Birmingham, Tufnell from Buxton and Utley and Bratley were local lads from Elsecar and Rawmarsh respectively.

The roads were thronged with people all the way from Worsbrough right to the town centre and the charabacs and people on bicycles were cheered as they came back, tired but happy.

When the team came back, Archie Taylor held the cup aloft all the way to the club's headquarters at the Clarence Hotel. Then suddenly the famous trophy was knocked from Taylor's grasp. It dropped beneath the feet of a horse, but apparently little damage was done to the cup.

At the reception at the Clarence, the Reverend Preedy was given the match ball, which was later returned to the club on his death in 1928 at the age of 65.

The net income from the cup ties was over £8,000 of which £4,339 2s 6d was received from the FA as the share of the semi-final and final ties. The profit on the year was £5,833 and the club was placed in a reasonably good financial position, though nearly £5,000 had already been earmarked for further stand and ground improvements.

10

Barnsley v Fulham

6 March 1920

Football League Division Two
Oakwell, Barnsley
Attendance: 6,000

Barnsley 4 Fulham 1
Wainscoat (3) Banks
Gittins (pen)

For this Easter Monday game against Fulham, the Reds made three changes from the team which drew 0–0 at Leicester on Saturday. George Donkin was fit again and returned on the right wing with Frank Smith, moving to inside right in place of Bill Fryer.

New player, twenty-one-year-old Russell Wainscoat, who was signed the previous Thursday from Maltby Main, was surprisingly handed the number ten shirt, with Harry Bell being dropped to accommodate him. Not surprisingly his quick elevation to first team status after a few trial games had created a good deal of interest in the town. The first time he touched the ball he got a good reception from the Maltby contingent and he quickly impressed with his pace and excellent control.

When Barnsley took up the running after Fulham had tested the Barnsley defenders, Wainscoat was in the limelight and after fifteen minutes made it a dream debut with the Reds' first goal. From a right wing corner by Donkin, Wainscoat was first to the ball and glided a fine header past the keeper to put his side in front.

The men from Fulham resumed with keen determination, and but for fine defensive work by Bethune and Tindall, they might have drawn level. Gittins then skimmed the crossbar with a beauty, and Halliwell shot high over the bar. However, seven minutes from the interval Barnsley's efforts were rewarded. Wainscoat placed a beautiful ball down the left for Dobson, took the return, and hammered the ball high into the net to send the fans into raptures.

Half-time: Barnsley 2 Fulham 0

To give Fulham their due, they never lost heart. They tackled their work in the

Russell Wainscoat, one of Barnsley's best ever players and the only one to score a hat-trick on his debut.

second half with zest, their forwards were always on the look out for opportunities, and with the advantage of the breeze they made it hard work for the Barnsley defenders. So persistent were Fulham that at the end of twenty minutes they had reduced Barnsley's lead with a good goal from Banks, but this only roused Barnsley to greater activity. Donkin made many good attacks on the right, and it was from one of these that gave Wainscoat the opportunity to notch a superb hat-trick on debut. Donkin centred with precision, and the young man from Maltby glided a first time effort into the net with the coolness and confidence of a veteran.

Wainscoat was now causing the Londoners all sorts of problems and it was no surprise when he took possession some twenty yards from goal, wormed his way past several defenders and just when he looked like scoring his fourth, he was fouled and a penalty was awarded. Wainscoat was urged to take the kick himself, but declined, so Gittins stepped up to hammer the ball home like a rocket to seal a fine performance by the Reds and in particular Russell Wainscoat.

That was the last thrilling incident in an action packed game and one which sent all the Barnsley fans home happy. At the final whistle the fans tried to get to Wainscoat to congratulate him and to carry him from the field, but he already had been ushered away by his delighted team mates. His wonderful display gave great satisfaction to the party of Maltby enthusiasts who had come to watch him. The Barnsley players, directors and staff extended their congratulations to him, which he accepted in a very modest way.

But praise was also due to the other Barnsley fellows who had worked with him. The forwards as a line showed an excellent understanding, with Donkin, Dobson and Halliwell all showing to good effect. The play of the half-back line, Fletcher, Gittins and Williams was a strong factor in Barnsley's command of the game. Gittins was another Barson, Fletcher another Boyle and Williams was a rare worker. As for those in the rear, Bethune fairly captivated the crowd with his improved display. He was safe and strong, Tindall fully maintained his good reputation, and what Cooper had to do he did it well, except that one goal which had him beaten all the way.

Result: Barnsley 4 Fulham 1

Barnsley: Cooper, Bethune and Tindall, Fletcher, Gittins and Williams, Donkin, Smith, Halliwell, Wainscoat and Dobson.

Russell Wainscoat

Russell still holds the record of being the only player to have scored three or more goals on debut for the Reds.

He was one of the all-time great Barnsley players, an inside forward who could create and score goals. He had wonderful ball control, was a brilliant dribbler and, along with Ernest Hine, the most popular player at Oakwell between the wars.

He had five seasons at Barnsley, from March 1919 to December 1923, when he was transferred to Middlesbrough for a fee of £4,000, a huge amount in those days. Indeed it is only in recent times that the actual fee was made known, for Barnsley would not disclose it at the time of his transfer.

At Oakwell he netted 56 goals in 153 league and cup games, before starring both for Middlesbrough and Leeds United, for whom he notched 86 goals in 215 matches.

He finished his career with Hull City, and was capped for England in 1929 against Scotland, whilst playing with Leeds.

Season: 1919/20

P	W	L	D	F	A	PTS
42	15	17	10	61	55	40

Division: Two
Position: Twelfth
Manager: Peter Sant
Top Scorer: Joe Halliwell (20)

11

Barnsley v South Shields

9 April 1927

Football League Division Two
Oakwell, Barnsley
Attendance: 2,290

Barnsley 6 South Shields 1
Eaton (5)   Oxberry
Fletcher

Despite the fact they had to face the wind and the rain, Barnsley started the game in excellent style. They nearly notched a goal before Shields had time to look around, Fletcher striking the upright with a fierce shot. This rousing raid confirmed that the Reds were in one of their old desperate moods, which bring forth goals, but although they kept on attacking they found it exceedingly hard at first to drive the leather home. Fletcher, however, missed one good chance when within close range; he lofted the ball yards over the bar. When the Shields' attack got possession they were nothing near so dangerous as the Barnsley front line and their best efforts so far came from Matthewson and Scott, who were

Frank Eaton (dark shirt, centre) secured a place in Barnsley's record books by becoming the first player to score 5 goals in a league game. Signed from New Mills in 1925, he scored 61 goals in 155 appearances before joining Reading in 1930.

exceedingly lively on the wings. It was obvious however, that Shields were adopting the wrong methods for the conditions underfoot.

Eighteen minutes had elapsed when Fletcher opened Barnsley's account from a centre by Curran, Brough making no mistake this time with a shot which nearly broke the net. Eaton notched Barnsley's second after 37 minutes with a beautiful shot which completely deceived the defence. Then came Barnsley's third goal, which was the easiest of the lot, easy because of the good work of Curran and Brooks, who played a big part in this success. Brooks led off with a powerful shot which the custodian, Taylor saved at full length, and Curran returned the leather across the unguarded goal, and Eaton practically walked the sphere into the net. This was the extent of the scoring in the first half, the nearest approach to a goal by Shields being a strong shot by Oxberry which went over, and another good effort by Scott, the leather going wide.

Half-time: Barnsley 3 South Shields 0

On the resumption, Shields, despite the wind, showed up much more promisingly, and after Parker had tested Gale with a red hot volley, Hird, from a free kick, skimmed the woodwork. Gale was also called up by Scott, who shot with marked precision for Gale to bring off a miraculous save. Barnsley appeared to have eased up somewhat, but ultimately they got into their stride again, and three more goals came in quick succession from Eaton. The first of these followed a lovely centre by Brooks, Eaton converting, and to score the next, Eaton smartly took advantage of a miss-kick by a defender, and dribbling on, finished with a brilliant volley which completely beat Taylor. The sixth goal was of a similar character but an even better effort as Eaton cleverly disposed his opposing back and left him standing still.

Naturally, this rate of scoring pleased the spectators immensely, and they yelled for another, but to no avail - there were no further goals for Barnsley. However, Shields rallied to such an extent as to reduce the margin by one and nearly got two more. Firstly, Loftus headed against the upright, then Oxberry scored with a shot which Gale partly stopped, but the ball was adjudged to have rolled over the line. Just before the end of the game, a penalty was given against Baines, but Gale made a magnificent save beating out a ferocious spot kick from Hird.

The game had been a test of endurance, and in this respect the Reds came out on top. The Oakwell defence was too strong and nippy for the Shields' attack, who were also slow in taking chances. As a team Barnsley were faster, more enterprising and the forwards far more deadly at close quarters.

Eaton was undoubtedly the hero of the day, and in scoring five goals in a league match created a club record. Eaton found the net a sixth time, but that did not count. Moreover, there was no fluke about any of the goals, and by his constructive play and distribution, he proved an ideal pivot, and has certainly solved the centre forward problem, which has been a source of anxiety to Barnsley for some time.

The Barnsley front line worked together splendidly, both the left and right wing being full of go, and they were admirably supported by the three hardworking halves, Allen, Caddick and Baines, who seemed to revel in the mud. In the rear, the backs, Dixon and Hodgkinson, and keeper Gale also played their part, in what had been a fine team performance.

Result: Barnsley 6 South Shields 1

Barnsley: Gale, Dixon and Hodgkinson, Allen, Caddick and Baines, Curran, Fletcher, Eaton, Tilson and Brook.
South Shields: Taylor, Wilson and Phizachlea, Metcalf, Hird and Trotter, Matthewson, Oxberry, Parker, Loftus and Scott.

Referee: Mr H P Hinderer (Newton Heath)

Frank Eaton

Frank joined the club from Derbyshire non-league team New Mills in September 1925. He was a consistent scorer for the Reds, notching 61 goals in 155 games, and benefited from the wing play of Jimmy Curran and Eric Brook, and the midfield promptings of Brough Fletcher and Fred Tilson. He stayed at Oakwell for five years, until his transfer to Reading in June 1930 for an undisclosed, but substantial fee. Eaton made 101 appearances for the 'Royals', scoring 33 goals, before ending his career with Queens Park Rangers in the 1933/34 season.

Season: 1926/27

P	W	L	D	F	A	PTS
42	17	16	9	88	87	43

Division: Two
Position: Eleventh
Manager: John Commins
Top Scorer: Frank Eaton (21) and Jimmy Curran (21)

12

Barnsley v Sheffield Wednesday

24 January 1931

FA Cup Fourth Round
Oakwell, Barnsley
Attendance: 24,032

Barnsley 2 Sheffield Wednesday 1
Harvey, Curran   Ball

For Sheffield Wednesday's first ever cup tie at Oakwell, the home fans were hoping that the game billed as David v Goliath, would turn out in favour of David.

Wednesday, First Division Champions in the previous two seasons, were currently top of the First Division, three points in front of their nearest rivals Arsenal, and going for a unique League and Cup double. The game therefore presented the Reds with their biggest challenge for nearly twenty years since they won the FA Cup.

Barnsley were without their regular goalkeeper Tommy Gale, and had to rely on the inexperienced second string keeper Len Crompton, who had made his first team debut the previous week against Charlton Athletic.

After four minutes' play a fine run and centre by Burgess enabled Allen to make a brilliant header, which Crompton parried splendidly. For some fifteen minutes or so, Wednesday were well on top and it appeared that it was only a question of time before the Champions would lay the foundations of victory.

Jimmy Curran, scorer of Barnsley's winning goal. He notched 73 goals in 256 appearances for the Reds, including 21 goals in 40 games during the 1926/27 season, still a season's record for a winger.

It was noticeable, however, that Crompton and his backs showed no signs of nerves. They were not overawed by the fame of the opposition. They pegged away and with Henderson a rock at centre half, and covering well, Wednesday's forwards could not find a way through.

Barnsley, having survived the critical first twenty minutes or so settled down to play some fine football and nearly took the lead when Harvey, with only goalkeeper Breedon to beat, somehow completely miss kicked from only six yards out.

Shortly afterwards, Wednesday thought they had scored when Hooper got the ball into the net, but the referee disallowed it for handball. In the build up, the Reds had also appealed for offside against outside left Rimmer, who had crossed the ball with the linesman flagging vigorously, the referee seemingly ignoring his flag.

Barnsley meanwhile had settled down and now began to get their forwards moving, with wingers Gibbs and Curran getting the better of the Wednesday full backs, Walker and Blenkinsop.

After 36 minutes, Harvey atoned for his earlier miss when he put the Reds in front. Winger Gibbs receiving a fine pass from Caddick, made headway down the left, turned inside Walker and delivered a superb centre which Harvey leapt to bullet a brilliant header past a stranded Breedon into the net.

The Wednesday had now become rather ragged in their movements, and their forwards were never together. Disconcerted by the vigorous tackling of the Barnsley defenders, they lost steadiness and seemed to have no plan of campaign.

Half-time: Barnsley 1 Sheffield Wednesday 0

On the resumption it was evident that the Reds, who were facing a gale force wind, were determined to hang on to their lead, rather than go in search of more goals. However, it was a policy which allowed Wednesday to have a much greater possession of the ball and they were never long out of the Barnsley quarters. They were continually striving to break through, but the Reds battled on and stood on no ceremony. Their policy was to get the ball out of their penalty area as quick as possible, and several times the ball finished high in the stands, or into touch. At centre half, George Henderson was playing the game of his life, working like a lion and continually heading the ball away from the danger area. Caddick showed Hooper no mercy, whilst Rimmer on the other wing found it difficult to find a way past Dixon. Indeed if a Wednesday man beat his opponent, he found a second and even a third man in his way. A tendency to play too close did not help the Champions, yet halfway through the second half they equalised, when Ball escaped Henderson for the only time in the game to plant a header past Crompton from Wilson's cross.

The goal however, rather than deflate the Oakwell men seemed to spur them on, and within minutes had regained the lead. Away went Gibbs, and Curran taking possession from the wingman, raced clear of the Wednesday defence. Breedon left his charge, but Curran took aim with a deliberation that made the home supporters' hair rise, lest he should be overtaken and robbed, and drove a rising ball into the top corner of the net.

The visitors had some fight left, but the Barnsley defence never yielded an inch and against the waves of Wednesday attacks stood solid, in their determination to snatch an unlikely, but brilliant victory. The whistle sounded and Barnsley had won because there was more of the joy of the game in them, more of the mood that wins.

Remembering the fact that he must have known that Barnsley enthusiasts had not too much confidence in him, Crompton deserves congratulations. In only his second game he had been magnificent, and the Oakwell supporters not only gave him a splendid ovation, but carried him off the field shoulder-high at the end.

To attempt to individualise in the Barnsley side would be to detract from the merits of a victory which was gained by team work from front to back. Every man pulled his weight in what had been Barnsley's most famous victory since their splendid cup win in 1912.

Finally a word of congratulations for the referee for his handling of a difficult, but not unpleasant game.

Result: Barnsley 2 Sheffield Wednesday 1

Barnsley: Crompton, Dixon and Richards, Smith, Henderson and Caddick, Curran, Proudfoot, Wallbanks, Harvey and Gibbs.
Sheffield Wednesday: Breedon, Walker and Blenkinsop, Strange, Leach and Wilson, Hooper, Burgess, Ball, Allen and Rimmer.

Referee: Mr P Snape (Blackpool)

Season: 1930/31

P	W	L	D	F	A	Pts
42	13	20	9	59	79	35

Division: Two
Position: Nineteenth
Manager: Brough Fletcher
Top Scorer: John Wallbanks (11)

13

Barnsley v Crewe Alexandra

12 December 1932

Football League Division Three North
Oakwell, Barnsley
Attendance: 1,350 Receipts: £55

Barnsley: 7 Crewe Alexandra 1
Andrews (3)   Swindells
Wallbanks (3)
Whitworth

Two days previously, on Saturday 10 December, the Reds turned in one of their worst performances for years, going down 2–1 to New Brighton, who were anchored at the bottom of the league. Consequently, Manager Brough Fletcher made six changes, one positional. Right back Ernie Robinson was dropped with Welshman Anuerin Richards recalled. The complete half-back line of Roland Happs, Tom Lockie and Harry Swaby were discarded and George Lax, George Henderson and Ernie Whitworth installed at right half, centre half and left half respectively. In the forward line, outside right Wilf Wadsworth was dropped, Teddy Ashton moving over

Harold Andrews (left) and John Wallbanks are still the only two Barnsley players to have scored a hat-trick for Barnsley in the same match. Andrews scored 44 goals in 116 fixtures (1932-35) and Wallbanks scored 65 goals in 126 appearances (1929-33).

from outside left with George Owencroft filling the number seven shirt.

The re-arranged Reds took a little time to settle down, but once they had found touch, they worked together with an admirable understanding. It was easily evident that the new half-back line would make their presence felt, and it was refreshing to see them take such a strong hand in the attack as well as keeping a tight hold of the Crewe invaders. Very early Crewe sent out a warning that they meant business and at this period the Oakwell defence had hardly got going properly, the fleety Crewe forwards often causing them anxiety. Swindells, their leader, was a most dangerous customer, and it was he who had the honour of opening the scoring with a ground shot which had keeper Tom Lynch well beaten. That was sufficient to remind Barnsley of their responsibilities, but as watchful as they were, Swindells would have done the same trick again if Lynch had not come to the rescue. One could not help but be impressed with the way the Crewe forwards worked together, but as raiders Barnsley were stronger and looked like scoring the equaliser anytime.

Seven minutes after Crewe's opening goal, John Wallbanks levelled the score with a very fine shot, and in another few minutes put Barnsley in front. By this time every member of the Oakwell side was on their mettle, and with the forwards taking the nearest route for goal, there were thrills galore at the Crewe end. Now and then Crewe responded with a promising burst, but the home defence, like the attack, had warmed to their work, and there were no further goals against the Reds. At half time Barnsley had four to their credit, but for good goalkeeping and ill-luck when the ball cannoned off an opponent or missed by inches, the Reds would have several more. Andrews put on Barnsley's third goal, taking full advantage of a weak return by a defender, and the same player registered the fourth when, from a corner, he netted with one of the best headers Oakwell had seen for some time. That was extent of the scoring up to the interval, but before that the Crewe keeper greatly distinguished himself when he smothered a shot from Smith and dealt with a header from Wallbanks. Barnsley, at this stage, looked well set for a big win.

Half-time; Barnsley 4 Crewe Alexandra 1

On the resumption, Crewe made a spirited attempt to alter the state of the scores, but with Barnsley so well balanced and the forwards in such a hungry mood for goals, the visitors had to play second fiddle. For the rest of the game Barnsley were bang on top, the only question being as to how many goals they would win by. After the Crewe keeper had cleared in miraculous fashion from Smith, and Lax had missed by inches, Whitworth gave Barnsley 'nap hand' scoring with a terrific drive. Wallbanks then completed his hat-trick with a header, the score then equalising Barnsley's previous best crop of goals this season when they scored six against Mansfield in October. That feat was surpassed, however, for Andrews emulated Wallbanks in performing the hat-trick, making Barnsley's total seven.

Most of the changes had worked admirably, the coolness and calculated methods of the middle line, and the firmness of the defence, with Lynch very confident in goal. Richards revealed much of his old form, Shotton showed a decided improvement, and Henderson was a dominating figure at centre half. Whitworth also impressed with a masterly display and Lax completed a very sound trio. In the forwards, Ashton's return to outside right was strikingly effective, which strengthened the view that after all, this is his proper position. He was speedy, forceful, and centred well, most of the goals coming from his good work. Of the others in the forward line, a special mention is due to both Andrews and Wallbanks, the former being the outstanding player on the pitch.

Result: Barnsley 7 Crewe Alexandra 1

Barnsley: Lynch, Richards and Shotton, Lax, Henderson and Whitworth, Ashton, Smith, Wallbanks, Andrews and Owencroft.
Crewe Alexandra: Foster, Pringle and Lawson, Ward, Keenor and Turner, Weale, Deacott, Swindells, Featherby and Mather.

Referee: Mr H M Camp (Derby)

Comments

The game produced two records which still stand today. First of all, the gate of 1,350 was and still is the smallest home gate since Barnsley became members of the Football League in the 1898/99 season. Secondly, to date, it is the only occasion in the club's league history that two players (Andrews and Wallbanks), had scored hat-tricks in the same match.

Season: 1932/33

P	W	L	D	F	A	Pts
42	19	15	8	92	80	46

Division: Three North
Position: Eighth
Manager: Brough Fletcher
Top Scorer: John Wallbanks (20)

14

Accrington Stanley v Barnsley

3 February 1934

Football League Division Three North
Peel Park, Accrington
Attendance: 2,814

Accrington Stanley 0 Barnsley 9
                    Blight (4), Spence (2)
                    Smith, Andrews, Ashton

In the first half the Reds were fully extended, Stanley's forwards showing neat combination, with Seedham particularly clever, and repeatedly paving the way for attacks on the Barnsley goal.

The Barnsley backs, Cookson and Shotton, however, proved equal to their task, but Henderson roused the ire of the spectators by perpetrating several fouls in his determination to stop Stanley's centre forward, Kelly.

Barnsley's attacking movements were more incisive than those of Accrington. Playing down the slope, Blight and Smith each scored in the first half, yet Stanley had played so well that it was expected that with the change of ends they would wipe out the arrears.

Half-time:
Accrington Stanley 0 Barnsley 2

In the second half, the Barnsley attack, by brilliant combination and clever play,

Abe Blight arrived at Oakwell in July 1933 and scored 36 goals in only 45 games in season's 1933/34 and 1934/35. A bad knee injury in the match against Notts Forest ended his career (Dec. 1934).

bewildered the Accrington defence, and in twelve minutes they increased their lead with four more goals.

The Stanley defence collapsed completely before the smart passing of the Barnsley forwards, ably assisted by the wing half backs, Bernard Harper and Ernie Whitworth. The Barnsley left wing pair of Harold Andrews and Teddy Ashton were prominent in most of the attacks and they completely bewildered Armstrong, the Accrington right back. As the second half got under way, the other Barnsley flank pair of Dicky Spence and Jackie Smith were equally the masters of Corcoran, the Stanley left back, and both wingers played so well that they made scoring so very easy. All through the second half, the Reds forwards wove their way past the dispirited Accrington defenders with consummate ease and it was merely a matter of whom should apply the finishing touch.

Not only did Barnsley end up scoring nine goals, but they had two or three amazing misses as well. Smith, once after walking to within three yards of the goal, tamely placed the ball in the keeper's hands, and Andrews fired over when equally well placed. They also did net the ball on two other occasions, but the goals were disallowed for off-side. Whilst the crowd were annoyed at the total eclipse of Accrington, they were forced to admire the brilliant play of the Barnsley forwards, particularly Dicky Spence. The outside right could do no wrong, his blistering pace and trickery had left back Corcoran turning this way and that, and the Stanley defender must have been a very relieved man at the final whistle. Although Spence only scored two of the Reds' goals he had a hand in five others, and Peel Park had seldom seen such a scintillating display as the Platts Common youngster served up. Of the other goals, Abe Blight notched up four, and Smith, Andrews and Ashton also got on the score sheet.

Result: Accrington Stanley 0 Barnsley 9

Accrington Stanley: Patterson, Armstrong and Corcoran, Dodds, Stoddart and McCulloch, Jeasons, Lennox, Kelly, Leedham and Clare.
Barnsley: Ellis, Cookson and Shotton, Harper, Henderson and Whitworth, Spence, Smith, Blight, Andrews and Ashton.

Note

As Barnsley scored six against Accrington at Oakwell earlier in the season, they amassed 15 goals in the season, which is still an aggregate record against any club in the same campaign. The nine goals scored is an away record for the Reds, and equalled the earlier feat of scoring nine goals against Loughborough in 1898/99, the debut league season for the club. The total league goals scored in 1933/34 (118), is still a record for a league season. Abe Blight's 31 goals was also a club record and stood until 1950/51, when Cecil McCormack netted 33.

It was also a season when the Reds bounced back into the Second Division, breaking a number of records along the way. They had gone 21 games undefeated, had broken every record the club ever had: undefeated at home throughout the season, highest number of goals ever scored in a season, greatest number of points ever obtained on opponents' grounds, highest individual goal-scoring record, and five forwards, each of whom reached double figures in goal-scoring. Apart from Blight's 31 goals, Dickie Spence and Tubby Ashton netted 19 each, closely followed by Harold Andrews with 18 and Jackie Smith with 12.

Season : 1933/34

P	W	L	D	F	A	Pts
42	27	7	8	118	61	62

Division: Three North
Position: Champions
Manager: Brough Fletcher
Top Scorer: Abe Blight (31)

15

New Brighton v Barnsley

5 May 1934

Football League Division Three North
Sandey's Park, Wallasey
Attendance: 8,460

New Brighton 0 Barnsley 1
                    Spence

Although Chesterfield had led the table for most of the season, there could be no denying the Reds the right to be on top at this vital stage of the season. After their 2–0 defeat at Wrexham on the last day of December 1933, they had gone 21 games without defeat, winning 16 and drawing 5, amassing an incredible 37 points out of a possible 42.

Second in the table Chesterfield were playing Stockport County, who were in third position, and any one of the three teams were still capable of winning the title, depending on the result of the two games, but Barnsley knew that victory would give them the Championship.

The Reds were still without their influential inside right, Jackie Smith, who had been injured at Halifax a fortnight earlier, his place being taken by Eddie Fleetwood; otherwise, they had their strongest team available.

Barnsley lost the toss, and were resigned to kicking up the considerable slope and into a strong wind. In the first few minutes, goalkeeper Tom Ellis took a six-yard goal kick which went to the halfway line. It was at once returned by

Dick Spence was a dazzling winger who departed Oakwell for Chelsea in 1934 and won two England caps whilst at Stamford Bridge. He was born at Platts Common and scored 25 times in 66 games for the Reds.

New Brighton centre half Amery, and the strong wind took it over Ellis's head, but fortunately for the Reds, it clipped the top of the bar before going for a goal kick.

The early part of the first half belonged to New Brighton, the Barnsley goal having several narrow escapes. Centre forward Davis missed badly on two occasions, the first he sent in a shot which hit the post, rebounded to him and with the goal at his mercy, he then drove the ball back to hit the other post. He then missed a simple header from a fine centre from outside left Pegg, when keeper Ellis misjudged the cross. However, after 16 minutes and against the run of play, Barnsley took the lead. Inside right Fleetwood, taking a pass from Harper, dribbled round McPherson and sent a beautiful ball to Dickie Spence. The winger sped round two defenders, and from fully 25 yards, unleashed a tremendous shot which flew past goalkeeper Bradshaw into the net.

Ten minutes later, Fleetwood and Spence co-operated in a movement which ended with Abe Blight driving the ball into the net. The New Brighton players at once protested that Blight was offside, and the referee, who had pointed to the centre without hesitation, consulted his linesman. He then disallowed the goal, not on the grounds that Blight was offside, but because Spence had fouled a New Brighton defender.

Then at the Barnsley end, there was a goalmouth scramble during which a New Brighton forward put the ball into the net, but fortunately for the Reds, the referee blew his whistle for a foul on Henderson.

Half-time: New Brighton 0 Barnsley 1

With a goal lead and the wind and slope in their favour, Barnsley had the game well in hand, but although their goal was not severely threatened as it had been in the first half, New Brighton still gave them some anxious moments. In the last quarter of an hour the Reds became more prominent in their possession and Blight nearly added a second goal with a first time shot which beat goalkeeper Bradshaw, but just went the wrong side of the upright.

Never at any time in the match had Barnsley produced their recent form, and the honours certainly had to go to the defence, who despite having a gruelling ordeal, held firm to the end. At the final whistle both the Barnsley team and their supporters, for whom there was about 3,000, went wild with delight. The team had remained unbeaten for 21 games, the title was theirs and they were now back in the Second Division.

Result: New Brighton 0 Barnsley 1

New Brighton: Bradshaw, Ratcliffe and Carr, Smedley, Amery and McPherson, Liggins, Allen, Davis, Butler and Pegg.

Barnsley: Ellis, Cookson and Shotton, Harper, Henderson and Whitworth, Spence, Fleetwood, Blight, Andrews and Ashton.

After the Match

The scenes at Liverpool were mild compared to the reception which awaited the team on their return to Barnsley. When the players reached the Royal Hotel, the club headquarters, the crowd were chanting for manager Brough Fletcher and the players, who soon appeared at the open window. 'Thank you very much,' said Fletcher. 'It is a great night for us, but while we are thinking of our own success, do not let us forget the losers. Stockport and Chesterfield, have made a great fight, and while we are glad we won, we must feel for them this evening.'

There is no doubt that Barnsley deserved their success. As already noted, they had gone 21 games without defeat, and had also broken every record that the club had: undefeated at home throughout the season, highest number of goals ever scored in a season (118), greatest number of points ever obtained on opponents' grounds (23), highest individual goal-scoring record (Abe Blight, 31), and five forwards each reached double figures in goal scoring. Apart from Blight, Dickie Spence and Tubby Ashton notched 19 each respectively, Harold Andrews scored 18, and Jackie Smith 12.

16

Birmingham City v Barnsley

15 January 1936

FA Cup Third Round Replay
St Andrews, Birmingham
Attendance: 34,000 Receipts: £2,218

Birmingham City 0 Barnsley 2
                    Hine, Waring

Barnsley, who were unlucky not to win at Oakwell, made no mistake in the replay at St Andrews, when they triumphed by two goals to none.

The achievement of the Second Division side was an excellent one, more so when it is borne in mind that only once this season had First Division Birmingham been beaten on their own ground.

The Reds made one change from the first game, Fred Fisher taking the place of the unfit Bob Thomas at outside right.

Barnsley immediately employed direct methods, and straight away there was a crispness about their work which suggested that they would give a good account of themselves.

After only five minutes' play, Barnsley nearly took the lead, when following a long throw from half back Tom Holley, Waring turned to hit a great shot that just went over the bar. Early exchanges saw the Reds in command of the play, and after only nine minutes Birmingham were reduced to ten men, when unfortunately, they were deprived of the services of outside right White. The capable winger, who had scored an excellent first minute goal when the teams met at Oakwell, was quickly in the picture by reason of his dashes down the wing. He was again making progress when Topping disposed him, and in the tackle White fell. He was carried off the field on the back of the Birmingham trainer and it transpired that he had sprained a ligament in the ankle. It was tough luck for Birmingham.

Barnsley quickly adapted themselves to the difficult conditions underfoot. The two inside forwards, Gallacher and Hine posed early problems by keeping the ball on the ground, and both had early shots which were not far off their target. In the 27th minute, Barnsley took the lead, following persistent work by Waring. From another throw in by Holley, the centre forward took the ball up the line, resisted the challenge of Hughes, and got across a delightful centre. Hine collected the ball and hit it powerfully from 15 yards through a crowd of players high into the net, giving Hibbs in the Birmingham goal no chance.

Half-time: Birmingham City 0 Barnsley 1

The second half began as the first had finished, with Barnsley well on top. The half-back line of Holley, Henderson and Harper were giving the Birmingham forwards little room to manoeuvre and Ellis in goal had little to do but to stop a couple of long range efforts. On the frost bound pitch there were mistakes, the ball often bouncing awkwardly, but Barnsley's players seemed more disposed to take risks, and the whole team were working hard.

The second and decisive goal came 14 minutes from the end, and quite extinguished whatever hopes Birmingham had of saving the game. Following a partial clearance by Fillingham, in checking Ashton, the ball went to Waring,

who promptly fastened on to it, ran forward a few yards, and from outside the penalty area, delivered a splendid shot. The ball swerved into the top corner of the net and had Hibbs beaten all the way.

After that second goal, Barnsley were all over their opponents, Hine, Waring and Gallacher indulging in some smooth passing which had the Birmingham defenders running here and there.

Hine was outstanding throughout. He played a

Ernest Hine is still the record goalscorer at Oakwell, with 131 goals in 307 appearances that spanned two spells with the Reds. He gained six England caps, scoring 4 goals, whilst with Leicester City. Apart from Tommy Taylor he was arguably the Reds' best ever forward.

great game in the match at Oakwell, and in yesterday's struggle he was always working the ball cleverly. Moreover, he covered a great deal of ground, frequently falling back to help his defence when Birmingham's forwards were moving in a menacing manner. He had valuable help from Waring and Ashton and they combined to trouble the Birmingham defenders throughout the game. Waring had never failed to score against Harry Hibbs in his Aston Villa days and kept up his record in this game.

Barnsley's half-back line was magnificent. With a light ball on a fast ground it was certainly a matter of speculation whether Henderson would be able to hold Jones, but as a matter of fact, the Birmingham leader was never a serious threat, so well did Henderson play. On either side of him were Holley and Harper, who revelled in their work, and Topping and Shotton at full-back stood firm on the few occasions that the Birmingham wingers threatened.

Birmingham were seen to best advantage in the second half, and although they forced several corners, Ellis in the Reds' goal had only one scare when Topping headed off the line. At the other end, Hibbs in the Birmingham goal had no chance with the goals, and indeed distinguished himself, making several fine saves from several goal bound efforts.

Result: Birmingham City 0 Barnsley 2

Birmingham City: Hibbs, Barkas and Hughes, Stoker, Fillingham and Loughran, White, Govenor, Jones, Harris and Guest.
Barnsley: Ellis, Shotton and Topping, Holley, Henderson and Harper, Fisher, Gallacher, Waring, Hine and Ashton.

Referee: Mr H S Shaw (Hull)

Season: 1935/36

P	W	L	D	F	A	Pts
42	12	21	9	54	80	33

Division: Two
Position: Twentieth
Manager: Brough Fletcher
Top Scorer: Ernest Hine (14)

17

Barnsley v Stoke City

15 February 1936

FA Cup Round Five
Oakwell, Barnsley
Attendance: 40,245 Receipts: £2,572

Barnsley 2 Stoke City 1
Gallacher   Davies
Hine

Everything you could wish for in a football match, happened in this game. Both teams played crisp, pulsating football, putting every ounce of skill and enthusiasm into their work.

An early goal is the dream of every side in a cup tie, but although Barnsley obtained one within 30 seconds of the kick-off, it did not play the important part in their glorious triumph that it might have done, for Stoke were on level terms in the sixth minute.

Barnsley's first goal, however, will go down in history, for it was the result of a movement which left the First Division side standing. Hine started it with a long pass over to the left wing, and Ashton put the ball inside to Waring. The former Villa player veered out to the left, and a clever back-heel found Ashton,

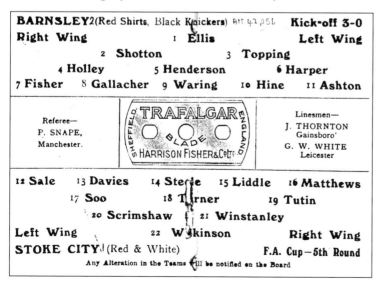

The teams' line-ups, taken from the programme of the Barnsley v Stoke City FA Cup fixture of 15 February 1936. Barnsley FC

Barnsley's team before the FA Cup match against Stoke, 15 February 1936: (back row, left to right) G Holley (trainer), T Holley (RH), R Shotton (RB), T Ellis (G), H Topping (LB), G Henderson (CH) and B Harper (LH); (front row, left to right) F Fisher (OR), F Gallacher (IR), P Waring (CF), E Hine (IL), T Ashton (OL) and B Fletcher (manager).

who had nipped inside. Ashton lofted the ball across the goalmouth and Gallacher running in headed into the net.

And so Stoke City's defence, which had not been pierced in four previous games, capitulated in the first minute at Oakwell. It was a movement, however, which would have beaten any defence.

For a few minutes Stoke were stunned, but they pulled themselves together and Davies equalised after six minutes. Harper and Topping both went for a ball which either of them could have disposed of comfortably. They collided and fell to the ground, and were still there when the ball rolled to Davies. He was fully 25 yards out and there was nothing terrific about his shot, but it was good enough to beat Ellis who was late going for it.

Although a setback for Barnsley, Waring and Hine soon started to dominate the Stoke defenders, particularly Waring. The part he had played in the Barnsley goal seemed to perplex the Stoke defence. They had placed Turner to deal with the Barnsley leader, but the latter had refused to stay put, for he was in the inside left position when he gave Ashton that critical and unorthodox pass.

Feeling that something would have to be done about it, Stoke put three men to watch Waring and one saw their uncertainty when he was about betrayed by some streaky kicking, particularly on the part of the full backs. Waring trailed his shadowers all over the field, and eventually we saw him doing not least effective work at right half, with Holley in the centre and George Henderson as a very definite third back.

A minute before the interval, Barnsley took the lead once again, and needless to say Waring was instrumental in setting up the goal. He slipped the ball to Ashton, and it seemed that the winger would fail to gather it, but he recovered and tapped it to Hine. There could only have been a streak of daylight through the packed defence, but straight and true went Hine's low shot just inside the post.

Half-time: Barnsley 2 Stoke City 1

Within minutes of the restart, Barnsley nearly added to their lead, when Waring shot over an open goal when Stoke goalkeeper Wilkinson misjudged a cross from Fisher. When Stoke attacked they found Ellis in tip-top form. He saved brilliantly from Liddle and then from Steele, and then made the save of the match from Matthews. Everything seemed lost when the ball came to Matthews, but Ellis sized up the situation, came out to narrow the target, and as he shot he anticipated the direction and his body was there to divert it for a corner.

Topping evidently had made up his mind that the best way to prevent being beaten with the ball by Matthews was not to allow the winger to get to it, so with fine anticipation he ran in front of Matthews and breasted the ball away and then thrust it up the field with a clear, clean kick every time.

It was from one of Topping's clearances at the expense of Matthews that Barnsley missed the easiest chance of the match. After taking the ball from the winger, Topping came through with it and then punted the ball up-field. It dropped just to the left of the goal, Gallacher rushed to it, brought it under control and found the Stoke backs so far away that he had only Wilkinson to beat. It was the easiest of chances, but the Barnsley man, trying to pass the ball gently into the net, only succeeded in lifting the ball into the hands of goalkeeper Wilkinson.

Barnsley tackled their work in the second period with much relish, and on one occasion Ashton came flying towards goal when he was brought down by Winstanley. The referee Mr Snape had controlled the game admirably, but for some reason did not give the penalty, to the surprise of all the 22 players and the crowd.

It was only in the last 20 minutes, when Barnsley adopted a 'what-we-have-we-hold' approach, that Stoke came into the match. They had every man in the goal hunt, leaving only Winstanley and Wilkinson to hold the fort. But Barnsley's defence stood firm, although there was an ominous moment when Henderson conceded a free kick just outside the penalty area.

A shrewdly packed goal, however, averted disaster, and a few minutes later the whistle blew the all clear, some minutes after the impatient (and anxious) Barnsley spectators had been sending up shrill appeals for 'time'.

Barnsley had many big players in the match. Topping as stated looked after Matthews well, while alongside him Shotton, the more experienced and more polished, held Sale effectively. Henderson dominated the centre of the field, and Steele found few opportunites to show his worth, whilst Holley and Harper at wing half added constructive work to their untiring efforts in defence. The tall young Holley, cool as an iceberg, used the ball always to effect, and although some of Harper's passes went astray, he was always a grafter.

Two players stood out in attack, Hine and Waring. In cleverness and capacity for work they were streets ahead of any of the Stoke forwards, and Hine, whom Barnsley launched on a splendid football career, played as well as when he was in his best days. The hard shooting inside left schemed to great effect and passed with perfect accuracy. He fetched and carried from no mans land and was continually prompting movements.

Waring was shadowed by two or three other players until the second half, but when he moved to inside right, he took on a roving role, and in the last hectic minutes he was right back in defence. He still however, had time to pose many problems for Turner, the Stoke centre half.

Gallacher played his part well, and Barnsley's slight weakness was on the wings. Ashton was not as prominent as usual and Fisher was often out of position. Both, however, were triers of the highest order.

The win took Barnsley further in the cup in any season since they won the trophy in 1912, and the attendance of 40,245 and receipts of £2,572 were ground records at the time. Indeed the ground attendance is still highest official figure for a game at Oakwell.

Result: Barnsley 2 Stoke City 1

Barnsley: Ellis, Shotton and Topping, Holley, Henderson and Harper, Fisher, Gallacher, Waring, Hine and Ashton.
Stoke City: Wilkinson, Winstanley and Scimshaw, Tutin, Turner and Soo, Matthews, Liddle, Steele, Davies and Sale.

Referee: Mr P Snape (Manchester)

18

Barnsley v Wrexham

8 April 1939

Football League Division Three North
Oakwell, Barnsley
Attendance: 14,988

Barnsley 2 Wrexham 1
Calder,   Burditt
Asquith

There were joyous scenes at Oakwell, where Barnsley's victory over Wrexham gave them promotion back to the Second Division and eventually the Division Three North Title. The Reds had gone 18 games without defeat, and although Wrexham gave them a tough game, Barnsley were worthy winners at the end of 90 minutes.

They made Barnsley fight every inch of the way, and with Barnsley's defence less convincing than usual, only brilliant goalkeeping by Binns prevented the visitors from taking an early lead. The crowd of 14,988, rose to him, when Wrexham left-winger Burgon shot well to the keepers left, but he dived full length to turn the ball away, for Harper to clear.

It was a narrow escape for Barnsley, and after enjoying the better of the early exchanges, they eventually took the lead. Bullock raced down the right wing, outpaced the Wrexham full-back Bellamy, and centred for Calder to slide the ball past Poland in the 28th minute. Indeed Wrexham's Welsh international goalkeeper had plenty of opportunities to show his capabilities. He caught several high shots, positioned well, and showed good judgment in running out when his backs were in difficulties.

However, in the 38th minute, the visitor's outside right Williams sped away from Logan and Everest to cross perfectly for centre forward Burditt to easily beat keeper Binns from close range to register the equaliser.

Poland then had luck on his side when he came out to collect a loose ball, but lost possession. Bullock gave the ball to Calder, whose shot struck Bellamy's legs and went out for a corner.

Half-time: Barnsley 1 Wrexham 1

Barnsley's 1938/39 squad with the Division Three (North) Championship Shield: (back row, left to right) Angus Seed (manager), Bernard Asquith, Norman Brunskill, Clifford Binns, Jack Everest, Jack Calder, Gordon Pallister and Tom Ratcliffe; (front row, left to right) Frank Bokas, Bob Shotton, Emlyn Williams, Bernard Harper (capt), Johnny Logan, Johnny Steele and Johnny Lang;(sat, left) George Bullock and Danny McGarry (sat, right).

At the beginning of the second half, Barnsley should have taken the lead, when Bullock cut inside Bellamy and hit a full-blooded drive, but fortunately for Wrexham the ball struck Lang and flew over the bar. Lang had taken the place of Steele, who was Barnsley's only ever present, but stood down in consequence of a slight knock received in yesterday's game at Stockport County. Normally an outside left Lang, although in an unaccustomed position, got some clever passes to his colleagues, Bullock being the main benefactor.

Williams, down the Wrexham right, caused the home defence some concern. Quick on the ball, his centres often threatened danger, and on one occasion, his cross was headed hopelessly wide by inside left Adamson.

McGarry should have given the Reds the lead when he endeavoured to tap the ball into the net, when a few yards from goal, but it struck full-back Tunney, and when Calder sent in a delightful shot the ever watchful Poland helped it over the bar. The ensuing corner, however, paved the way to the deciding goal. Bullock dropped another centre in front of goal, and Asquith's smart header was out of Poland's reach.

Logan, who broke up many attacks, was twice injured and on the second occasion, a few minutes from the end, was assisted off the field.

Harper and Brunskill, however, showed resolution and with Calder, Bullock and Asquith leading raids on Wrexham's goal, there was always a possibility that Barnsley would increase their lead.

However, Poland stood firm in the Wrexham goal, and despite the odd scare or two the game finished with no more goals.

Result: Barnsley 2 Wrexham 1

Barnsley: Binns, Williams and Everest, Brunskill, Harper and Logan, Bullock, Lang, Calder, Asquith and McGarry.
Wrexham: Poland, Tunney and Bellamy, Savage, Snow and Bellis, Williams, Nelson, Burditt, Adamson and Burgon.

Season's Comments

Supporters who watched the 1938/39 team, were convinced that they would have achieved promotion from Division Two in 1939/40, if the war had not intervened. Most of them also felt that it was the best team between the wars and probably, the best in the Reds' history.

They had good players all through the side, and several brilliant ones in Bernard Harper, a centre half of international class, who played for England in a war-time international and centre forward Bernard Asquith and outside right George Bullock. Indeed if Bullock had not been killed during the war, there were those who thought he would have followed other Oakwell wingers such as Mordue, Wall, Brook and Spence in playing for England.

The team failed to score in only two games, suffered only five defeats, (still a club record for a league season), and scored 94 goals and conceded only 34 (another club record for least goals conceded in a season), and both were a record in all four divisions that season. All five regular forwards also got into double figures, Asquith (28), Steele (17), McGarry (12), and Bullock and Lang (10 each).

These goals were also the main reason why the Reds won 30 league games, a statistic which is still a club record for wins in a season.

Season: 1938/39

P	W	L	D	F	A	Pts
42	30	5	7	94	34	67

Division: Three North
Position: Champions
Manager: Angus Seed
Top Scorer: Bernard Asquith (28)

19

Barnsley v Newcastle United

10 January 1946

FA Cup Third Round 2nd Leg
Oakwell, Barnsley
Attendance: 30,000

Barnsley 3 Newcastle United 0
Wilson, Smith,
Baxter

This game will go down as one of the epics in Barnsley's great cup fighting history, not only because of their fine victory, but also because of their classic display.

Barnsley's performance was all the more amazing for it was under conditions which supplied the severest test: a heavy ground, a strong wind, and rain for most of the game. Also, it was against one of the teams who were favourites for the cup.

They were also faced with the herculean task of giving a team of the calibre of Newcastle United a two goal start in the second instalment of their tie, Barnsley having lost the first leg at Newcastle by 4 goals to 2.

Barnsley adopted the right tactics from the start. Having the good

Johnny Kelly. A very skillful outside-left, Johnny was an amazing dribbler of the ball. Signed from Greenock Morton in December 1945, he made 229 appearances for Barnsley, scoring 26 goals. He also played twice for Scotland, against Wales and Northern Ireland, in 1948.

fortune to win the toss, which gave them first half advantage of a sweeping wind, they realised the necessity of an early goal if their chances were not to evaporate altogether. They immediately surged forward on the attack with rare vim, and got their rewards after only 14 minutes. Following a corner, Joe Wilson, the Barnsley centre half and captain, scored with a grand hook shot. Almost immediately they had the ball in the net again, but Johnny Kelly was given offside, running forward to net at the far post from a cross from Gavin Smith. However, 4 minutes later, they were on equal terms on aggregate. Newcastle goalkeeper King knocked out a shot from Jimmy Baxter, the ball went to Smith, who, taking careful aim from an acute angle, steered the ball into the far corner of the net.

After 33 minutes the Reds should have been in front in the tie. Inside right Roy Cooling sent in a powerful shot which beat King all ends up, but left back Corbett dived to save a certain goal with his hands, a save which would have done credit to a goalkeeper. However, Gordon Pallister's spot kick was too near King and the keeper punched the shot out with his right fist, to keep Newcastle on level terms.

Barnsley had been so much on top in the first half, that goalkeeper Harry Holdcroft handled the ball on only one occasion, and then only when Wilson passed the ball back to him.

Half-time: Barnsley 2 Newcastle United 0

Barnsley's whirlwind methods in the first half however, had apparently disorganised Newcastle and when they had their turn with the wind, the Reds still did more of the pressing. True, Barnsley's goal did eventually have one or two narrow escapes, making the crowd hold their breath, and Holdcroft saved well on a couple of occasions.

With the game heading for extra time, and only five minutes of normal time to go, the crowd went wild with delight. Newcastle goalkeeper King made his only mistake of the match, when he badly misjudged a shot of no great power from Barnsley inside left Baxter, and the ball ended up in the net to give the Reds a remarkable win by 5 goals to 4 on aggregate.

When a team plays like a machine, each part has to be perfect. But while all the Barnsley players contributed to the fine win, two players stood out for masterly displays: Johnny Kelly and Joe Wilson.

Kelly was irrepressible, time after time, he beat two or three men with perfect dribbles, and his centres invariably threatened danger.

Neither Harvey or Cowell could do anything with him as he wove his way along the wing and into the centre. He was a winger of the quality of a Matthews, and already a Scottish international, destined for many more caps.

Wilson's play inspired his side. He was a captain in action as well as word. No one worked harder, and he had the Newcastle and England centre forward Albert Stubbins 'in his pocket' all afternoon.

Result: Barnsley 3 Newcastle United 0 (Aggregate score 5–4 to Barnsley)

Barnsley: Holdcroft, Cunningham and Pallister, Mansley, Wilson and Logan, Smith, Cooling, Robledo, Baxter and Kelly.
Newcastle United: King, Cowell and Corbett, Harvey, Smith and Crowe, Milburn, Taylor, Stubbins, Clifton and Hair.

Referee: Corporal A Ellis (Snaith)

Season: 1945/46

P	W	L	D	F	A	Pts
42	17	14	11	76	68	45

Division: North War League
Manager: Angus Seed
Top Scorer: George Robledo (15)

20

Huddersfield Town v Barnsley

11 January 1947

FA Cup Third Round
Leeds Road, Huddersfield
Attendance: 39,994 Receipts: £4,944

Huddersfield Town 3 Barnsley 4

Doherty (2)	Smith, Asquith
Bateman	Bennett, Baxter

A superb piece of opportunism by Jimmy Baxter, Barnsley's diminutive inside left, who was playing with a cracked jaw, scored the goal which beat Huddersfield Town and put Barnsley in the fourth round of the FA Cup. Barnsley deserved their victory, gained through hard, fast, and well conceived football, which had Huddersfield gasping in the last half hour.

The result was football of a quality which must have made their game the best of the whole round, and victory was undoubtedly due to teamwork, not individual brilliance. Incident followed incident, with such rapidity throughout the game that even spectators were breathless, and the ball was kept moving on the ground with real precision.

Barnsley hustled First Division Huddersfield right from the start and the pass back to Hesford, which Town liked to exploit, was foiled by the persistent attentions of Robledo and Bennett.

Baxter was prominent with a beautiful through pass, which Robledo seemed certain to take when he was brought down by Hepplewhite, but Pallister's free kick was too high.

Barnsley's first goal in 7 minutes was brilliantly conceived. Pallister's pass to Bennett was hooked to Robledo, who returned the ball to the inside right, and Hesford made a desperate one handed save from his shot. However, the ball ran loose and Smith was on hand to put the ball in the net before Hesford could recover, despite the obliqueness of the angle.

Within three minutes, Town were on level terms. Pallister gave away a free kick from which Doherty raced through, while Barnsley appealed for offside, and headed a goal as Rimmington challenged. Barnsley protested, but the referee refused their request to consult a linesman and the goal counted.

Asquith headed over a free-kick by Morris, who was certainly deputising well

Scorer of the winning goal, Jimmy Baxter was one of Barnsley's best ever all-round footballers. A diminutive schemer, he played in 263 games and scored 59 goals during two periods with the club. He also played for Preston alongside Tom Finney and appeared in the 1953/54 FA Cup Final versus West Bromwich Albion.

for Johnny Kelly, and a desperate clearance by Bailey saved Town, and caused Smith to receive attention. Tom Wilson, the Barnsley trainer and Huddersfield's former centre half and captain, was given a special cheer when he raced on the field to attend to the Barnsley winger.

Metcalf was allowed to race through while Barnsley appealed for offside, but he pushed the ball too far forward and Rimmimgton was able to clear.

However, after 34 minutes, Barnsley fell in arrears, the goal seemed to be due to the fatal delay of Rimmington's challenge and to the anticipation and quick moving of Peter Doherty. Bateman's centre was breasted down by Doherty, but the ball ran away from him towards Rimmington, who could successfully have smothered it then, instead of waiting until Doherty recovered possession to score from about four yards.

Two minutes before half-time the brilliance of four men brought an equalising goal. Robledo and Bennett cleverly took the defence away from the goalmouth as Smith was about to take a corner. Smith placed it precisely into the resultant open space, and Asquith anticipating the move, ran in to head well wide of Hesford. It was a planned goal, and those responsible for its working moved with split-second perfection in timing, and their positioning was equally accurate.

Before half time Baxter drove a ball just wide, after Hesford had run out to clear from Smith, a narrow escape for Town, and a warning Hesford was not to heed. But Hesford saved Town just on half-time when he got a hand to a terrific Smith drive.

Half-time: Huddersfield Town 2 Barnsley 2

Barnsley were behind for the second time in the game, in the 48th minute, due to a magnificent centre from the touchline, whilst running at full-speed by Metcalf. Rimmington leapt for it, missed it and the ball rebounded from the crossbar where Bateman just beat Pallister to it and pushed it into the net.

This galvanised Barnsley into a fight-back and in one hectic spell Hesford saved from Baxter, Smith shot inches wide, Hesford snatched a free-kick from Morris's head, and two corners were cleared.

In the 68th minute, Bennett equalised for Barnsley, and the goal was a real thriller. Put through by Robledo, he found great speed to ward off two defenders converging on him, and, as Hesford advanced, he drove the ball into the net with terrific force, a magnificent effort.

Robledo and Smith were a constant threat to Town, and Bennett just failed to reach a superb pass from Smith and then Hesford caught another centre from Bennett, before Baxter's brilliance brought the winning goal after 78 minutes.

The cleverness of Asquith gave Baxter his opportunity 25 yards from goal, and he quickly realised Hesford was off on the six-yard line and promptly lobbed the ball over him and into the roof of the net. Hesford made a desperate effort to reach the ball, but it was perfectly placed just under the bar, and Baxter can be forgiven his war dance of delight.

Barnsley's supporters (between 3,000 and 4,000), expressed their jubilation in a volume of cheers, rattles and motor horns, quite the equal anything the Town partisans had hitherto produced.

Result: Huddersfield Town 3 Barnsley 4

Huddersfield Town: Hesford, Bailey and Stewart, Barker, Hepplewhite and Boot, Bateman, Glazzard, Rodgers, Doherty and Metcalf
Barnsley: Rimmington, Cunningham and Pallister, Glover, Wilson and Asquith, Smith, Bennett, Robledo, Baxter and Morris.

Referee: Mr A Meadows (Redcar)

Season: 1946/47

P	W	L	D	F	A	Pts
42	17	17	8	84	86	42

Division: Two
Position: Tenth
Manager: Angus Seed
Top Scorer: George Robledo (23)

21

Barnsley v Luton Town

9 September 1950

Football League Division Two
Oakwell, Barnsley
Attendance: 21,964

Barnsley 6 Luton Town 1
McCormack (5)   Jinks
Wright

Those 'on the carpet' through passes to Barnsley leader Cecil McCormack paid big dividends at Oakwell on Saturday. Not only did McCormack score five brilliant goals, but he completely bewitched, bothered and bewildered a floundering Luton defence and his speed, craft and devastating shooting ability in this match will

definitely be remembered by all who were present, and who were treated to the best football feast for many years.

It is a long time since the Reds have had a centre forward of McCormack's calibre who could display such masterly ball control and completely demoralise defenders with a neat flick, a deft feint or a body swerve, performed with lightning precision, and then round off this neat work with picture goals.

Cec McCormack was a post-war Oakwell legend, with 33 league goals in only 37 appearances in the 1950/51 season. Altogether he notched 43 goals in 51 games before his transfer to Notts County in November 1951.

Cec McCormack pictured scoring his fifth goal against Luton Town.

If Barnsley are favoured with dry grounds throughout the season and they can maintain this high speed football there is every indication that first division football will be played in the 1951/52 season.

On present day form there are very few teams in the Second Division who will overcome this powerful all-round Barnsley eleven. They convincingly outplayed Luton that it would have been no surprise had the Reds score reached double figures.

Throughout the game Baxter and Blanchflower supplied a stream of judicious passes to the front line, and the diminutive Baxter in particular was a will-o-the-wisp, being here, there and everywhere.

Luton's forward line was never in the picture and their two inside forwards, Taylor and former Newcastle player Stobbart, were so busy assisting the harassed defence to stem the continual Barnsley onslaughts they had no time to get their own forwards moving.

The visitors' centre forward, Jinks, who obtained his sides consolation goal was a lively leader, but was well held by Arthur Glover, making his first appearance in the senior side this season, deputising for Kitchen who injured an ankle in the Brentford match.

McCormack who had led Owen, reputed to be one of the best centre halves in the Second Division, a merry dance, waltzed round him in the 14th minute and was preparing to shoot when tripped by Lake. The referee had no hesitation in awarding a penalty and the Barnsley leader scored his third spot-kick for his new club.

From then onwards, Barnsley piled on the pressure and after 27 minutes the goal hungry McCormack fastened on to a centre from Johnny Kelly, and with a lightning body swerve rounded Owen and finished with a glorious left foot drive from 18 yards, which left goalkeeper Hughes helpless.

Three minutes later, Alex Wright put the Reds three up, hooking in a perfect cross from Gavin Smith, before Jinks pulled a goal back for Luton, five minutes before half-time.

Half-time: Barnsley 3 Luton Town 1

Throughout the second half the tired Luton defence could find no answer to elusive McCormack who scored three further goals, bringing his season's tally to 13 and thus becoming the country's leading goal scorer.

A goal which will be remembered was McCormack's third after 55 minutes. Jimmy Baxter, who had halted one of the rare Luton raids, dashed down the field for fifty yards, evaded the challenge of two Luton defenders before finally despatching a perfect through pass to the waiting McCormack, who outwitted Owen and Lake to shoot past the advancing Hughes from an awkward angle.

By scoring five goals, McCormack equalled a club record shared by Frank Eaton (v South Shields, 1926/27), Peter Cunningham (v Darlington 1932/33) and Beaumont Asquith (v Darlington, 1938/9).

At the conclusion of the game, McCormack received a well-deserved ovation.

Result: Barnsley 6 Luton Town 1

Barnsley: P Kelly, Bannister and Pallister, Blanchflower, Glover and Baxter, Smith, McMorran, McCormack, Wright and J Kelly.
Luton Town: Hughes, Cook and Lake, Watkins, Owen and Shanks, Glover, Stobbart, Jinks, Taylor and Wyles.

Referee: Mr S E Law (West Bromwich)

Season: 1950/51

P	W	L	D	F	A	Pts
42	15	17	10	74	68	40

Division: Two
Position: Fifteenth
Manager: Angus Seed
Top Scorer: Cecil McCormack (33)

Cecil McCormack

Cecil was one of the best post-war centre forwards to play for Barnsley, though his stay with the club lasted only fifteen months.

After playing for Gateshead and Middlesborough, he took himself out of league football to play for non-league Chelmsford.

In August 1950 he signed for Barnsley for £7,000, and in his second game for the Reds scored twice in a 3–3 draw with Hull City. Seven goals in his first five games, made him an instant favourite with the home fans and the five goals against Luton were the icing on the cake.

The diminutive centre forward had superb control, was quick and elusive, and all centre halves in Division Two, found him a handful.

In 51 games for Barnsley he scored 43 goals, and his 33 goals in 37 games in 1950/51 is still a club record. In November 1951 the club accepted an offer of £20,000 from Notts County for his transfer and he notched 35 goals in 82 games for the Nottingham team.

His last English club was Midland League King Lynn, before he finally emigrated to Canada.

22

Barnsley v Queens Park Rangers

4 November 1950

Football League Division Two
Oakwell, Barnsley
Attendance: 17,878

Barnsley 7 Queens Park Rangers 0
Taylor (3), McCormack (2)
Kelly, McMorran

Manager Angus Seed made only one change from the 2-1 defeat at Notts County, which meant a place for the 18-year-old soldier, Tommy Taylor, who took the place of the injured Jimmy Baxter at inside left. It was Taylor's second game for the Reds, having made his first team debut in the 3-1 win over Grimsby Town at Oakwell four weeks previously.

There was little signs early on of the goal avalanche that was to follow, as Queens Park Rangers in the first twenty minutes or so played some enterprising and entertaining football. They were well prompted by the hard working inside left Hatton, whose tricky footwork and ball control was an outstanding feature of the game.

Running Hatton close was the speedy Shepherd on the Rangers' left wing who was the only visiting forward who appeared capable of trying a shot. Shepherd was faced however by the robust Eddie Bannister who, with some fine, well timed tackles soon cleared the danger when the former Wombwell winger was sweeping through those wide open spaces.

Addinall, the Rangers spearhead, did not fare at all favourably against the resolute Arthur Glover who pounced on any loose ball like a ferret. To complete a compact Barnsley defence, skipper Gordon Pallister set about his task of subduing the opposing right wing with his usual calmness and although not having a great deal to do completely blotted out Wardle.

Goalkeeper Pat Kelly will rarely have had a quieter game this season. The only shots possessing any sort of sting in them at all came from Shepherd, but Kelly was usually well in the line of flight. Blanchflower and Normanton also did useful work in the Barnsley rearguard.

Barnsley opened the scoring after 27 minutes when Cecil McCormack put the Reds in front with a typical McCormack effort. In fact only Cecil could have got

Tommy Taylor is probably the most famous and one of the best centre forwards of all time. A tally of 28 goals in 46 games attracted all the top clubs in England and he was eventually transferred to Manchester United in March 1953 for £29,999. He soon became an England international, scoring 16 goals in 19 games, before being tragically killed in the Munich air disaster on 6 February 1958.

the ball into the net from such an awkward position. Johnny Kelly swung over one of his many perfect centres for the goalkeeper to dash out of his goal, but unfortunately he fumbled the ball and in a flash McCormack spun round and let drive in the same movement to hit the ball into the net like a jet-propelled rocket.

A minute later, Taylor scored his first Barnsley goal when he chased a ball down the middle, controlled it instantly and fired it low into the net as keeper Gullen raced out of his goal in despair.

Half-time: Barnsley 2 Queens Park Rangers 0

Five minutes into the second half, after 50 minutes, it was Eddie McMorran's turn to find the Rangers' net. Charging through the fray like a goal-crazed bull, the energetic Eddie cracked the ball home with a sparkling left foot drive which left Gullen helpless to register Barnsley's third.

Then came another two goals in a dizzy one minute spell midway through the second half, when Taylor had scored during a goalmouth scramble; then McCormack brought his season's total to 22 with a point blank shot from close in.

The dejected Rangers would have needed a line of tanks to have checked Barnsley after this, and more goals just had to come. They did, Tommy Taylor completed his hat-trick and sent the crowd wild with delight after 87 minutes, and Johnny Kelly, who played a storming game in the second half made it seven with the last kick of the match to bring his first goal of the season.

However, the star of the show had been the 18-year-old Taylor. It had been a magnificent performance by the Smithies youngster, who never put a foot wrong. His perfect distribution and thoughtful passes kept Johnny Kelly's twinkling feet fully occupied throughout the game.

In fact, Taylor and Kelly moulded together into a really effective left wing considering it was the first time they had played together.

However, although the youngster stole the show, Irish inside right Eddie McMorran's contribution had also been invaluable, his constant foraging and powerful running had given the Queens Park Rangers defence a torrid time all afternoon.

Rangers, while being a nippy side never knew what had hit them and although they served up some stream-lined approach work the forwards hardly ever looked like a goal.

Result: Barnsley 7 Queens Park Rangers 0

Barnsley: P Kelly, Bannister and Pallister, Blanchflower, Glover and Normanton, Smith, McMorran, McCormack, Taylor and J Kelly.
Queens Park Rangers: Gullen, Peppit and Heath, Nelson, Chapman and Farrow, Wardle, Mills, Addinall, Hatton and Shepherd.

Referee: Mr W R Rodgers (Birmingham)

Tommy Taylor

Tommy was probably the best known of any player to have played for the Reds, and one of, if not the best centre forward that England has ever produced.

During that first season, he notched 7 goals in 12 games, before going off to finish his National Service and in the 1952/53 season notched 21 goals in 30 games, before his transfer to Manchester United for £29,999 in March 1953.

He played 168 games for United, scoring 112 goals, and for England, 16 goals in 19 internationals, including a hat-trick in the 5-1 win over Eire.

Sadly he was one of 20 people who were killed in the 1958 Munich air disaster, at the still young age of 26.

He had tremendous strength, pace, two great feet and incredible power in the air. He was at the time of his death, the best centre forward in Europe, and would I believe, have become the best number nine of all time.

Barnsley v Sheffield Wednesday

16 February 1952

Football League Division Two
Oakwell, Barnsley
Attendance: 29,975

Barnsley 5 Sheffield Wednesday 4

Baxter (2, 1 pen)   Froggatt (2), Sewell,
Lambert (2), McNeil   Dooley

Barnsley's 'Derby' game with Sheffield Wednesday provided a real thriller for nearly 30,000 spectators at Oakwell.

There was something of everything, a game fought in a cup tie atmosphere, punctuated with some first class football, nine goals and finally a winning goal from a player who was virtually passenger in the closing minutes.

Both sides set off at a cracking pace, and it was not long before Wednesday's battering ram of a centre forward, Derek Dooley, was barging into the Reds' defenders like a wild bull. Dooley's play carried the stamp of crudity, and as far as he was concerned football finesse was a nonentity.

However, he found his master in Matt McNeil, the Barnsley centre half, who proved his superior by buttoning Dooley in his pocket and keeping him there by reason of vastly superior skill. He made the Wednesday forward look like the novice he was.

Barnsley opened the scoring with a fine right foot drive from Ken Lambert, normally a reserve player, who incidentally was born within a stones throw of Hillsborough at Southey Green, but Wednesday hit back with two goals in four minutes. After 20 minutes, inside right Sewell levelled for the Owls and four minutes later, winger Redfearn Froggatt scored the second to put Wednesday in front. Indeed Foggatt was causing a real threat to the Reds and it took a huge effort from the home side to get back on level terms. This they did minutes before half-time, with a well taken penalty from the Reds' star of the match, Jimmy Baxter, after O'Donnell had brought down Eddie McMorran.

Half-time: Barnsley 2 Sheffield Wednesday 2

Within four minutes of the restart, the Reds had taken the lead. Baxter was yet

Harry Hough was the regular goalkeeper throughout the 1950s and holds the record number of appearances for a Barnsley goalkeeper, 364 games.

again the marksman, scoring with a fine oblique shot which flashed just inside the far post, which keeper McIntosh would have been disappointed with, as he seemed well out of position.

The game continued to fluctuate and thrill and fortunes swung from one team to the other like a pendulum.

Unfortunately after 55 minutes, the Barnsley centre half, Matt McNeil was badly injured in a collision with Dooley, and had to be carried off the field on a stretcher. The Reds had to re-organise, with Tim Ward moving to centre half and Jimmy Baxter dropping back from inside left to left half.

In the 70th minute the Owls equalised with a goal from Froggatt, but the Wednesday fans' cheers, soon turned to groans, when a minute later, following a good cross from Gavin Smith, Lambert buried a fine header to put the Reds back in front once more. Three minutes later, in the 73rd minute, the match was turned on its head once again, when the rampaging Dooley turned in a cross from Froggatt to make it 4–4.

McNeil then returned to the field, moving out on to the left wing, with Pattison moving inside to accommodate him. However, McNeil's injury was obviously a bad one for he was limping badly, and was no more than a passenger.

It was now becoming a grim battle, and tempers got a little frayed towards the end. With only a few minutes remaining, Wednesday's fragile defence fell for the fifth and last time, and it was enough to seal victory for the Reds and two points in the bargain.

The Owls' defenders for some reason took their eye off the limping McNeil and it proved to be their downfall. From a cross from the right, McNeil was completely unmarked at the far post, but leapt superbly to rocket home a great header past McIntosh to seal a brilliant win for the Reds.

However, there was still time for the rampaging Dooley to crash into Barnsley keeper Harry Hough, and immediately it was obvious that he was hurt. As it was Hough had fractured his forearm and unluckily for him had lost the chance of playing for England 'B' against Holland 'B' a few days later.

The Barnsley team deserved their bonus, they all worked like Trojans, to make up for the injured McNeil. Indeed if the lanky centre half could have escaped injury, the result almost certainly would have been more decisive.

For Barnsley, apart from the hero McNeil, two players stood out like beacons: Jimmy Baxter and Eddie McMorran. Baxter's defence splitting passes caused no end of trouble to the Wednesday defence and he capped a marvellous display with two well taken goals. McMorran worked like a beever and gave O'Donnell an afternoon he would want to forget.

Result: Barnsley 5 Sheffield Wednesday 4

Barnsley: Hough, Farrell and Pallister, Ward, McNeil and Scattergood, Smith, Lambert, McMorran, Baxter and Pattison.
Sheffield Wednesday: McIntosh, Bannister and Curtis, Gannon, O'Donnell and Davies, Froggatt, Sewell, Dooley, Quixall and Woodhead.

Referee: Mr T W Rand (Easington)

Season: 1951/52

P	W	L	D	F	A	Pts
42	11	17	14	59	72	36

Division: Two
Position: Twentieth
Manager: Angus Seed
Top Scorer: Eddie McMorran (15)

24

Barnsley v Brighton & Hove Albion

10 January 1953

FA Cup Third Round
Oakwell, Barnsley
Attendance: 17,244

Barnsley 4 Brighton & Hove Albion 3
Taylor (2), Kaye,   Owens, Howard, Reed
McMorran

One of the greatest comebacks in the club's history occurred at Oakwell when the Reds came back from the dead, to win one of the most dramatic Cup ties of all time.

After 45 minutes of a pathetic first half display, a number of spectators decided they had seen their team humbled enough, and made their way home. How fitting it was then, that those so-called supporters should miss the best performance, the Reds have given this season.

Barnsley were soon shown by their Southern visitors that they were not going to have it all their own way. The Third Division team were soon producing fast, crisp, entertaining football, swung the ball about in workman-like fashion, and exploiting the tremendous turn of speed possessed by their diminutive outside left Howard, were constantly menacing the Barnsley goal area.,

After 22 minutes, with Medhurst clutching his stomach after stopping a McMorran pile-driver, Brighton slipped away and surprisingly took the lead, when centre forward Owens leapt into the air and rocketed a fine cross by Howard past the helpless Jack Walls.

What a tonic for the visitors and what a shock for Barnsley. Within 60 seconds, Brighton were two up, blond haired Howard heading the ball home from a perfectly placed centre by outside right Reed.

Somewhat dismayed at the thrust and energy of their opponents, Barnsley seemed unable to counteract the brilliance and speed of left winger Howard, who was the complete master of Blenkinsopp. It was from another of his centres that Brighton forged further ahead in the 35th minute, Reed sending an unstoppable shot past Walls to make it three.

Half time: Barnsley 0 Brighton & Hove Albion 3

Eddie McMorran was an Irish international before he joined the Reds in July 1950 from Leeds United. He scored 34 goals in 109 appearances, at inside forward or centre forward. He played 15 times for Ireland, 9 whilst at Oakwell, and joined Doncaster Rovers for £8,000 in March 1953.

Although the Barnsley defence had been unable to hold a very live wire Brighton attack, the home forwards had been dogged by ill-luck. Praiseworthy goal-scoring attempts by both Taylor and McMorran going only inches wide or over.

Hopes of a Reds' revival received a further setback when Blenkinsopp moved out to the right wing, Smith dropping to right back, Lumley to right half and Arthur Kaye to inside right. This move, however, whether necessitated by an injury or a strategic one on the part of Manager Angus Seed was instrumental in Barnsley's great recovery.

The moment that Norman Smith took over the full-back role, Howard, the instigator of the Brighton attacks was completely subdued. Instead of possessing a dynamic and devastating attack with the greater power on the wings, Brighton found they had a one-sided disjointed forward line, which floundered hopelessly without the brilliance of Howard.

Then in the 62nd minute the transformation commenced. With the ball running in their favour for the first time in the game, the four-pronged home attack swung into action in a fine methodical manner and, after a ball by McMorran had been partially cleared, Kaye sent a curling shot high into the net. Straight into the onslaught as soon as centre forward Owens played the ball, McMorran, who was releasing terrific drives from all angles, narrowly failed to reduce the arrears when his hard low shot was scrambled round the post for an unfruitful corner.

Barnsley hadn't to wait long however. Two minutes after McMorran's near miss, Tommy Taylor scored the Reds' second with a great shot. Receiving the ball from McMorran, the centre forward, although challenged by three defenders, beat Medhurst with a grand shot.

Fully realising that their team was capable of at least earning a draw, the Oakwell crowd yelled encouragingly. After both Kelly and Taylor had brought the best out of Medhurst with two full blooded drives, we once again saw a

The Barnsley squad, 1952-53 season (players only): (back row, left to right) Nomanton, Glover, Spruce, Youell, Allan, Hough, May, Walls, McNeil, Sharp, Jackson and Kelly (D); (middle row, left to right) Wood, Smith, Lumley, McMorran, Taylor, Kelly (J) and Ward; (front row, left to right) Jarman, Hamilton, Hudson, Thomas and Chappell.

period of Brighton attacking which, however, came to grief on the astute execution of the offside rule by the home defence.

Then it happened; Barnsley were on level terms. Holding off the challenge of a number of Brighton defenders, McMorran hurtled himself into a fine scoring position before releasing a shot which left Medhurst floundering on the ground.

With the crowd completely aroused, Barnsley were urged on by their roars. There was no stopping the Reds. After McMorran had been brought down as he was bursting through, Taylor headed the ball to the Irishman who blazed it across the goalmouth.

Full of enthusiasm, Barnsley battered away at the Brighton goal and in the 87th minute, came the all-important winner. Fittingly enough it was the best goal of the game. McMorran, abounding with energy, leapt high into the air to head down an Arthur Kaye cross into the path of Tommy Taylor, and the young centre forward moved forward to beat Medhurst with a glorious and powerful shot.

Oakwell erupted, anything the crowd could get their hands on went up in the air, the Reds' supporters realising they had just witnessed one of the most remarkable comebacks in the club's long and proud history.

Result: Barnsley 4 Brighton & Hove Albion 3

Barnsley: Walls, Blenkinsopp and Hudson, Smith, Archer and Normanton, Kaye, Lumley, Taylor, McMorran and Kelly.
Brighton & Hove Albion: Medhurst, Tennant and McLafferty, McIvenny, Walton and Wilson, Reed, Leadbetter, Owens, Bennett and Howard.

Referee: Mr C W Bucknall (Birmingham)

Season: 1952/53

P	W	L	D	F	A	Pts
42	5	29	8	47	108	18

Division: Two
Position: Twenty Second (Bottom)
Manager: Angus Seed
Top Scorer: Tommy Taylor (19)

25

Barnsley v Rochdale

3 May 1955

Football League Division Three North
Oakwell, Barnsley
Attendance: 11,606

Barnsley 2 Rochdale 0
Wood (2)

The Reds had secured promotion at Chester, winning 2–0, but the title was still to be played for when they entertained Rochdale, in their penultimate game of the season.

Accrington Stanley could still catch the Reds, so victory was vital against the 'Dale' if the title was to land at Oakwell.

Inside left Bobby Wood had not been 100 per cent fit for a number of weeks, and it was Manager Tim Ward's intention to give the young Scot a rest for this game. However, when the Barnsley chief saw his injury list mount up to eight men, he had no option but to continue to play the youngster.

At Chester, centre half George Spruce had broken his toe, which necessitated Henry Walter's moving to centre half, with Barrie Betts, normally a recognised right back playing left half. Lol Chappell was brought back at centre forward, with second top scorer Bobby Brown moving to outside left in place of Frank Bartlett.

The Rochdale game was Barnsley's tenth game in less than a month, and in the early stages it was apparent that the team were tired and a wee bit lifeless. Nevertheless, many of the 11,000 spectators must have been disappointed at times with their football, their movements lacked the enthusiasm one expected.

No doubt about one thing though, Barnsley dominated the game for almost the whole of the ninety minutes. But whereas their mid-field movements were invariably good enough to watch, the number of easy chances that were wasted by the forwards was astonishing.

Centre forward Lol Chappell was the main offender. His shooting was way off the mark and altogether he did not have a particularly happy match.

It must be admitted that Barnsley were forced to take the field with a much changed side because of injuries but the substitutes all aquitted themselves well.

Walters at centre half, kept a firm hold over Rochdale centre forward Gemmell and Bobby Brown, deputising for Frank Bartlett certainly introduced a better class of football on to the left wing.

Barnsley FC's team with the Division Three (North) Championship Shield: (back row, left to right) M Jackson, N Smith, J Thomas, G Spruce, H Hough, H May, J Jarman, H Walters and R Shotton (trainer); (front row, left to right) A Kaye, T Lumley, L Chappell, T Ward (manager), R Wood, R Brown and F Bartlett.

Young Barrie Betts, brought in for his first senior game in the left half position, was the instigator of the move which gave Barnsley their first goal after 28 minutes. He slipped a perfect pass to inside left Bobby Wood who drove the ball from fully 25 yards into the corner of the Rochdale net.

In the 80th minute after a glaring miss by Lol Chappell, Bobby Wood put the game out of Rochdale's reach by notching his and Barnsley's second goal to clinch the Championship for the Reds.

Result: Barnsley 2 Rochdale 0

Barnsley: Hough, Thomas and May, Smith, Walters and Betts, Kaye, Lumley, Chappell, Wood and Brown.
Rochdale: Morton, McCullough and Boyle, Lynn, Glover and Murphy, Kendall, Mitcheson, Gemmell, Black and Anders.

Referee: Mr J W Topliss (Grimsby)

The Season's Summary

In the end the Reds won the Championship by four clear points ahead of Accrington Stanley and, after their magnificent run, they fully deserved their success.

Barnsley skipper Norman Smith being presented with the Division Three (North) Championship Shield.

Scunthorpe, Accrington, York City and Hartlepool United all had their hour of glory, with Barnsley coming into their own at the right time to finish off the season with a truly remarkable run which brought 30 points out of a possible 34.

But for a recent defeat at Chesterfield, they would have gone 17 games without defeat, four short of the club record, achieved in the 1933/34 promotion season.

As it was they went 12 games without defeat, it was unlucky 13 against Chesterfield during which time there was a period when eight successive victories were notched without a goal being conceded.

At Wrexham they were defeated 3–0, at Barrow 3–1, and this gave Accrington Stanley a seven point lead in the table. However, the pressure that the Reds put on their rivals with their superb run during the last 17 games in which they scored 34 goals and conceded only 9 eventually told on Accrington, and put Barnsley back in the Second Division, a division which they class as their rightful home.

Season: 1954/55

P	W	L	D	F	A	Pts
46	30	11	5	86	46	65

Division: Three North
Position: Champions
Manager: Tim Ward
Top Scorer: Lol Chappell (21)

Cardiff City v Barnsley

26 January 1957

FA Cup Fourth Round
Ninian Park, Cardiff
Attendance: 31,919

Cardiff City 0 Barnsley 1
            Bartlett

Barnsley, struggling in the Second Division, were not fancied too highly at First Division Cardiff, and there was much optimism in the Welsh Valleys that this would be their year of reaching the twin towers of Wembley.

Cardiff wore the look of a First Division team who thought they could tame the Reds at their own convenience. Instead of going all out from the kick off, they pottered about with short passes rather than try to establish an early lead.

Barnsley, after a nervous opening, sensed the mistake their opponents were making and with skipper Henry Walters setting a magnificent example, launched the non-stop chase which completely upset Cardiff's timing and accuracy.

Indeed had all the chances been taken, Barnsley would have been well in front at half-time. After goalkeeper Vearncombe had stopped a brilliant shot from Arthur Kaye, the goalkeeper palmed down an effort from John Edgar (deputising for the injured Sid Storey), and had to dive backwards to stop it rolling into the net.

Harry Hough dealt efficiently with shots by young England centre forward Gerry Hitchens and right-winger Brian Walsh, whilst at the other end, Vearncombe's hesitancy nearly cost his side a goal. Inexplicably, he left a clearance to left back Ron Stitfall, who accidentally backheeled the ball in the crowded goalmouth and turned to see the ball trickling past the foot of the post for a corner.

Half-time: Cardiff City 0 Barnsley 0

In the second half, Barnsley were full of confidence and remained quicker to the ball and to the tackle. Cardiff tried frantically to find their gears, but when they did manage to break through, full-backs John Short and Colin Swift caught them offside or Hough was on his toes.

Frank Bartlett (8) played 325 games for the Reds and scored 80 goals between 1950 and 1963. A versatile player at wing-half or inside forward, he was the ideal club man.

The Barnsley half-backs had started to dominate play, and were now bringing into play the Reds' danger men, wingers Arthur Kaye and Johnny McCann. Both Kaye and McCann made the City full-backs look poor, and generally the home defence had little idea how to cope with them.

Although they lacked fire power, inside men Holmes, Chappell and Edgar battled for every ball and kept it moving to the flanks.

Cardiff tried to get the ball to their danger man, winger Walsh, but Colin Swift must take great credit for the way he practically played the right-winger out of the match. The left back invariably got to the ball first, and was successful in his tackles, playing one of the best ever matches for the Reds.

Wing halves Frank Bartlett and Henry Walters were superb. They cut out almost every challenge and kept the ball moving briskly to their own men. Walters set a fine example of tireless working. One move when he sold a dummy to Walsh brought the house down.

It was this service from defence which kept Barnsley so firmly in the picture. Frequently it made them look the superior footballing combination.

As Cardiff became more frantic at trying to find a way through the Barnsley defence, they came upon the immovable object by the name of Duncan Sharp. The centre half had looked a shade uncertain in the first ten minutes or so, but as the game wore on he was magnificent, completely dominating the dangerous

Gerry Hitchens. Indeed none of the Cardiff forwards relished the occasion when they were challenged by the tall centre half.

In the latter stages, the superior team work of Barnsley was much better than that of their opponents. There was more unity in the side and there was never any question of looking for a draw, even in the dying minutes.

Onwards they battled in search of the vital goal, and sure enough it came, three minutes from time. Arthur Kaye tantalising the Cardiff defence for the umpteenth time forced a corner on the right. He took it himself, Cardiff inside left Ron Stockin headed away, but the ball went straight to right half Frank Bartlett, who chested it down and, from just outside the penalty area in one lightning movement, shot on the volley. Goalkeeper Graham Vearncombe, whose view had been blocked by a crowd of players, dived too late to his left and saw the ball zooming under the crossbar to put the Reds into the fifth round of the cup.

Result: Cardiff City 0 Barnsley 1

Cardiff City: Vearncombe, Rutter and Stitfall, Baker, Malloy and Sullivan, Walsh, McSeveney, Hitchens, Stockin and Nugent.
Barnsley: Hough, Short and Swift, Bartlett, Sharp and Walters, Kaye, Holmes, Chappell, Edgar and McCann.
Referee: Mr A E Westwood (Stratford)

After Match Comments

Match Winner: Frank Bartlett, whose 87th minute goal was the match winner, said: 'Honestly, I took a chance with that shot. I breasted down the ball and let fly. You can imagine my excitement when I saw the ball in the net. It was too good to be true, because I had not seen a space in a line of blue shirts.'

Manager: Tim Ward: 'What pleased me as much as the result was how we played and the fact that we won strictly on our merits. Our lads worked hard for all of the 90 minutes and for much of the game, you would have thought that we were the First Division team.'

Season: 1956/57

P	W	L	D	F	A	Pts
42	12	20	10	59	89	34

Division: Two
Position: Nineteenth
Manager: Tim Ward
Top Scorer: Arthur Kaye (15)

27

Barnsley v Ipswich Town

4 September 1957

Football League Division Two
Oakwell, Barnsley
Attendance: 12,185

Barnsley 5 Ipswich Town 1
Kaye (3, 2 pens)   Siddall
Wood, Anderson

The first week of September 1957 will always be remembered as the Arthur Kaye week, for the little pocket dynamo who occupied the Reds' outside right position for most of the 1950s.

Prior to the Ipswich game four days earlier the Reds had eclipsed Derby County 4–1, when Kaye had tormented the Rams' defenders. He not only scored one of the goals, but created two more for centre forward Lol Chappell, with inch-perfect crosses and helping the number nine to notch his fifth hat-trick for the club.

Naturally Manager Tim Ward named an unchanged team for the Wednesday night visit of Ipswich, and the Reds quickly started off where they had left off at Derby, with a goal after only two minutes.

Kaye, for the first, but certainly not the last time of the evening, left the Suffolk team's left back Andy Malcolm tackling thin air as he sped away down the right wing to cross for right half Bobby Wood to hammer home from close range.

Indeed Wood had a splendid game throughout, as did Norman Smith, the ex-Arsenal player, who was normally a wing half, but who had been moved to the inside forward position earlier in the season by Tim Ward, and had rewarded his manager with some splendid performances. Smith openly admitted he preferred to play at wing half, but as a naturally attacking player, was equally at home in a more advanced position.

However, ten minutes later, Brian Siddall, the visitors' outside right broke through the home defence to net the equaliser. With the Barnsley defence appealing for offside, centre forward Blackman crossed from the left and Siddall, who was making his first team debut headed powerfully past Harry Hough in the Reds' goal.

Kaye continued to torment Malcolm and Elsworthy down the left hand side of the Ipswich defence and, after 34 minutes, supplied centre forward Lol

Chappell with a brilliant pass. Chappell played the ball square for inside right Eric Anderson to shoot past keeper Bailey, for his one and only goal for the Reds in his nine appearances for the club.

Three minutes later, right half Pickett, not knowing which way the Reds' left winger Johnny McCann was going, tripped him in the box to earn the Reds a penalty. Kaye quickly seized the ball, perkily bounced the ball on his head a few times as he walked up to place the ball on the spot, and proceeded to hammer the ball past a motionless Bailey to put Barnsley 3–1 in the lead.

Half-time: Barnsley 3 Ipswich Town 1

Soon after the restart, Chappell, full-back John Short and Bobby Wood all hit the woodwork as Barnsley dominated play.

Ipswich, although moving the ball around in midfield, never posed a serious threat to the home goal, and were constantly on the back foot when after 67 minutes Kaye got the ball and made yet another surging run. The little dynamo slipped past Elsworthy, Rees and Malcolm as if they were not there, and goalkeeper Roy Bailey had no option but to trip the winger. Needless to say, Kaye got up and blasted the penalty past Bailey for goal number four.

Five minutes later the Reds went nap for the first time for exactly twelve months. Lol Chappell, although not getting his name on the score sheet, but had worked hard throughout the game, supplied a fine pass to McCann, whose cross was played sideways by Wood, for the diminutive Kaye to drive past Bailey for what had been a brilliant hat-trick.

It had been a tremendous all round performance, but the icing on the cake had been the individual performance of Kaye. Not only for his goals, but for his complete destruction of the Ipswich defence, with his dribbling skill and electrifying pace.

Throughout the club's history, there cannot have been many better, if any, individual performances than Arthur Kaye's on this barmy September evening in 1957.

Result: Barnsley 5 Ipswich Town 1

Barnsley: Hough, Short and Swift, Wood, Sharp and Bartlett, Kaye, Anderson, Chappell, Smith and McCann.
Ipswich Town: Bailey, Carberry and Malcolm, Pickett, Rees (Dia) and Elsworthy, Siddall, Rees (Derek), Blackman, Millward and Leadbeater.

Referee: Mr L J Hamer (Bolton)
Season: 1957/58

P	W	L	D	F	A	Pts
42	14	16	12	70	74	40

Arthur Kaye was one of Barnsley's best ever wingers. A diminutive and competitive player, he had all the necessary skills, plus courage, determination and a love for his home town club. Unlucky not to win a full England cap, he did play for the Under 23 team and the Football League.

Division: Two
Position: Fourteenth
Manager: Tim Ward
Top Scorer: Lol Chappell (19)

Arthur Kaye

Arthur Kaye, as stated in my official history of the Reds, was my boyhood hero in the 1950s, because for me he personified all the good things in the game. He had ability of course, lots of it, but he also had all the other attributes that you associate with a great player: pace, dribbling skills, aggression, determination, commitment, a great shot, and he could cross a ball on to a sixpence. He also had a great loyalty to the club for most of his career at Oakwell. Those who saw him play will, I am sure, agree that it was a great injustice that he never won an England cap. He was without question the best player I have ever seen not to have won full international honours.

For the Reds he notched 60 goals in 280 games, represented the England Under 21 team, played for the Football League against the Irish League and was in the England World Cup Squad of 40 players for the 1958 World Cup in Sweden.

He also played for Blackpool and Middlesbrough and ended his career with Colchester United, for whom he helped win promotion in the twilight of his career.

28

Barnsley v Huddersfield Town

6 February 1961

FA Cup Fourth Round Replay
Oakwell, Barnsley
Attendance: 29,149

Barnsley 1 Huddersfield Town 0
Wood

Barnsley had already played six games in the Cup, beating Gateshead 2–0, after a 0–0 draw in the North East; Bradford City 2–1 at Valley Parade; and Reading 3–1, after extra time at Oakwell, after a 1–1 draw at Elm Park in round three. Incidentally, in the replay against Reading it was the first time, officially, that a cup tie had gone to extra time at Oakwell.

In the first game against Huddersfield in front of 44,761 at Leeds Road, Oliver put Barnsley in front, Coddington equalising with a dubious penalty. It was a match that the Reds deserved to win, and there was much anticipation awaiting the return game at Oakwell.

In the early stages, Huddersfield had the edge in midfield, with Dinsdale and Massie foraging and curbing the enthusiasm of Beaumont and Oliver.

But with more clear-cut openings, they had only young Bettany as a player with a shot, and stand-in goalkeeper Clarrie Williams (deputising for Don Leeson), who stated he would not let the side down, kept his promise with a number of top-class saves from the inside right.

As the first half wore on and with centre forward Bert Tindill always niggling in his efforts to set up shooting positions, and frequently drawing Coddington from the middle, ruffling the centre half into all sorts of indiscretions, Barnsley started to take a grip of the game and looked more likely to break the deadlock.

A few minutes before half-time, Barnsley took the lead, and it was no more than justice, following one of the most bad-tempered incidents Oakwell had seen in years, Ray Wilson being the culprit. Before the free kick from which Barnsley scored, Wilson had been guilty of three successive double-footed tackles, the sort one does not expect from public park players, let alone a man who was probably England's best left back.

Then, blatantly, Wilson obstructed Smillie as the right-winger tried to run the ball to the goal line. Referee Keith Howley awarded the indirect free kick, almost

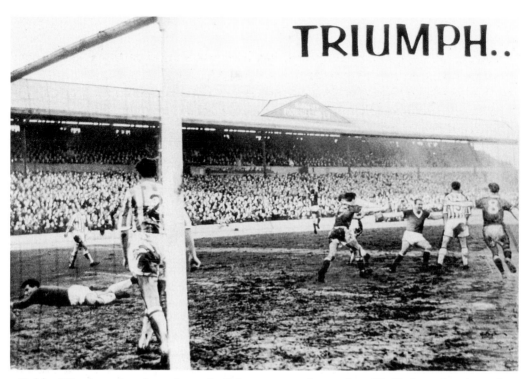

Bobby Wood scoring the only goal of the game on the stroke of half-time. Another of Barnsley's long-serving post-war players, Bobby made 373 appearances, scoring 44 goals in a career that spanned 14 years at Oakwell. He would have been the ideal midfield player of today.

on the penalty line, and Wilson lashed the ball angrily into the crowd behind the goal. It smacked a young girl in the face, and ambulance men and police were called by the referee. Mr Howley took out his notebook as he talked to Wilson. Play was held up for several minutes, during which Wilson went to the retaining wall where the spectator was being treated. Police ordered him away as spectators shouted and shook their fists.

Play restarted with Smillie taking the indirect free kick, the ball was lobbed into the middle, went out from a bunch of players to Bobby Wood, who running in quickly, to lash the ball low from the edge of the penalty area into the corner of the net.

It was fitting that Wood should score the goal, for with the heavy ground cutting speed of play more to his liking, was here, there, and everywhere, plugging gaps and sparking off attacking moves. He must have covered more ground than any other player in a tremendous example setting display that must rate his best for the club.

Half-time: Barnsley 1 Huddersfield Town 0

In the second half Wood continued to dominate the midfield, even when younger players like Houghton, Beaumont, and Oliver wobbled physically in the last 15 minutes, he kept going. He blotted out Balderstone, and gave part-timer Alan Green a hand in coping with the dangerous O'Grady.

Full marks to Green for sticking successfully to a thankless task. While alone, he rarely subdued O'Grady, but his persistence cut out the threat from the winger almost to nil.

On the other flank, young Eric Brookes was clever in possession and shrewd in timing tackles on McHale, yet he did not have a great match. A stronger, more determined McHale would have served his side better. Wolverhampton's Stan Cullis was one of a host of managers present to watch Brookes and O'Grady.

There were no frills about the work of Duncan Sharp, who tackled free scorer Derek Stokes out of existence. In fact, there were no worthwhile goal attempts from the centre forward, although he stood up well to the battering.

Long before the end Barnsley should have been in an unassailable position. In the last 15 minutes Frank Beaumont and Ron Smillie missed easy chances to put the game beyond any doubt.

In an hectic last 10 minutes, a desperate Huddersfield threw everything into attack and their best chance came when centre half Coddington, up with his forwards raced on to a headed pass glided by Bladerstone between Sharp and Green. But Williams capped a good afternoon's work with a diving save which also earned him a bruised chest and shoulder.

After that Barnsley marshalled forces with more determination than ever, putting so strong and realistic a barrier along their penalty line that Huddersfield could find no way through.

Result: Barnsley 1 Huddersfield Town 0

Barnsley: Williams, Green and Brookes, Wood, Sharp and Houghton, Smillie, Beaumont, Tindill, Oliver and Lunn.
Huddersfield Town: Fearnley, Parker and Wilson, Massie, Coddington and Dinsdale, McHale, Bettany, Stokes, Balderstone and O'Grady.

Referee: Mr K Howley (Middlesbrough)

Season: 1960/61

P	W	L	D	F	A	Pts
46	21	18	7	83	80	49

Division: Three
Position: Eighth
Manager: Johnny Steele
Top Scorer: Frank Bartlett (15)

29

Barnsley v Luton Town

18 February 1961

FA Cup Fifth Round
Oakwell, Barnsley
Attendance: 32,923 Receipts: £6,604

Barnsley 1 Luton Town 0
Lunn

It was the visitors who had the early chances, and the Reds had two lucky escapes when first Fleming, then Ashworth shot wide with only goalkeeper Williams to beat.

For the rest of the first half, mainly through their half-back line of Wood, Sharp and Houghton, the Reds took control and Luton's scoring chances before the interval were then negligible compared to the opportunities the Oakwell men had.

Three times in five minutes Oliver shaped to score. First he was robbed at the last second by Morton, then his header hit the crossbar and dropped out of play and finally he shot over the bar.

In the 31st minute, Luton had their biggest let-off, when Tindill's shot was stopped on the line by full-back Dunne, and on a number of occasions Luton were rescued by defenders clearing off or around the goal line.

Ten minutes before half-time, Standen made a flying save which was in the brilliant class, from a Billy Houghton 20 yard shot. During this first half, Barnsley had the bright sun behind them and when they failed to score before the interval it was generally thought that they might have 'missed the boat', and they must have thought they would never score.

Half-time: Barnsley 0 Luton Town 0

Barnsley missed a chance to clip Luton's wings long before they did, Frank Bartlett mis-hitting the ball from 10 yards in the 53rd minute. It was most unlike the reliable Bartlett. Three minutes later all Barnsley hearts missed a beat when right-winger David Noake put the ball in the net after Williams partially saved his first attempt. Referee Smith pointed to the centre circle to signal a goal, it couldn't be true thought the Oakwell crowd. Sure enough it wasn't; Barnsley

The Barnsley team, season 1960-61: (back row, left to right) C Swift, R Wood, D Sharp, D Leeson, W Houghton, D Barber; (front row, left to right) F Bartlett, R Smillie, F Beaumont, B Tindill, K Oliver, J Lunn, E Brookes.

brought to Smith's attention that the linesman had his flag up, the Luton players crowded round the referee, but he walked over to consult his linesman, and eventually gave a free kick for offside against Ashworth. There was a huge sigh of relief all round the ground.

Anyway, Barnsley were not put out of their stride, and in the 68th minute came the goal that the home side deserved, and it was created by the best player on the pitch, Billy Houghton. Houghton had been outstanding, both in defence and attack, and the pass he made inside full-back Dunne, was a magnificent ball. Jackie Lunn, the outside left fastened on to the ball and cut in for goal. Keeper Jim Standen quickly had to make up his mind whether to stay in goal or go out to meet Lunn, he plumped for the latter and the Barnsley winger instead of letting fly in his characteristic manner, calmly lobbed the ball over the stranded keeper and into the net.

Needlessly to say, Oakwell erupted, and although Barnsley made the mistake of going on the defensive after this, but, nevertheless, they twice had golden opportunities to increase their lead. In the 71st minute, Oliver shot wide from close range and 11 minutes from time, Bartlett raced 30 yards to goal with Bramwell hot on his trail, but ended by firing wide.

Luton forced corner after corner in a tension packed finish, but conceding a goal looked the last thing the Reds' defence would do. As a matter of fact they had conceded only four goals in their eight FA Cup matches.

Duncan Sharp so effectively stopped anything and anybody that came down the centre of the field and experienced centre forward Turner took to roving on the wing to escape his attention. Up front Bert Tindill's knowledge was a vital part of the success story, and Smillie, Bartlett and Oliver all had moments of sparkle.

Eventually the final whistle went and after over 12 hours of Cup football, Barnsley were in round six for the first time since 1936 and for only the fourth time since the club was formed in 1887.

Result: Barnsley 1 Luton Town 0

Barnsley: Williams, Swift and Brookes, Wood, Sharp and Houghton, Smillie, Bartlett, Tindill, Oliver and Lunn.
Luton Town: Standen, Dunne and Bramwell, Morton, Kelly and Groves, Noake, Ashworth, Turner, Brown and Fleming.

Referee: Mr R E Smith (Newport)

After Match Comments

Barnsley won fairly and squarely and matched Luton for football. So many Third Division Clubs have got through to the sixth round by what is loosely described as kick-and-rush methods. Barnsley are not among them. Luton Manager Sam Bartram sportingly backed up this statement by saying: 'Barnsley deserved to win. They played the better football and were like demons for all of the 90 minutes.' *(Yorshire Post)*

30

Barnsley v Leicester City

8 March 1961

FA Cup Sixth Round Replay
Oakwell, Barnsley
Attendance: 39,250 Receipts: £7,727

Barnsley 1 Leicester City 2
Oliver   Riley, Leek

Although the Reds defended stoutly at Filbert Street in the first game, with centre half Duncan Sharp outstanding, they had chances to win the match, which would have secured them a place in the semi-finals for the first time since 1912.

Barnsley players with the *Daily Mirror* Giant-Killers Cup: (left to right) Colin Brooks, Bert Tindill, Duncan Sharp, Billy Houghton, Colin Swift, Ken Oliver, Eric Brookes, Ron Smillie.

Ken Oliver (outstretching arms) scoring Barnsley's equalising goal against Leicester City, which sent the game into extra time. Oliver, signed from South Shields in March 1960, was one of the best headers of the ball to have played for the Reds. He notched 54 goals in 113 appearances.

In the ninth minute, after a great passing movement between Frank Bartlett and Bert Tindill, England Under 23 international goalkeeper Gordon Banks needed one of the best saves from his repertoire to stop a glorious hook shot from Ken Oliver.

Then with the second half only four minutes old, Ron Smillie crossed the ball to Tindill, who took careful aim at goal but headed just wide. Finally Oliver had the best chance of all in the 77th minute, when only eight yards out, he mis-hit a cross from Smillie.

But nevertheless, Barnsley's achievement at Filbert Street will go into the records as one of the club's greatest away performances.

For the replay in front of a packed Oakwell, both teams were unchanged from the battle at Filbert Street, four days earlier. Indeed many who were at the game, thought it impossible that there could have been a bigger attendance at the ground. However, official figures given for the match, suggest otherwise, but rumours abounded that the record attendance of 40,255 v Stoke City in 1936 had been beaten.

Within the first five minutes of play, the visitors had a remarkable let off when Smillie beat two men on the right and put the ball over to Oliver, who headed past

Banks, but saw the ball hit the inside of the post and rebounded into play again. The Barnsley players appealed that the ball had crossed the line, but they were turned down.

Referee Jack Kelly of Chorley also waved play on when the Leicester players appealed that the ball had gone over the Barnsley goal line in the 22nd minute. But the linesman flagged for a goal and Leicester were in the lead. The scorer was England Under 23 International Howard Riley, who played better than he did in the game at Leicester, but even so did not have a field day against the veteran-like 17-year-old Eric Brookes. Riley slammed the ball at goal from an oblique angle and it somehow squeezed past a nervy Leeson who quickly grabbed it a second time, but the ball had gone over the line said the linesman.

Before Leicester had much time to celebrate, the Reds were on level terms, and deservedly so. A centre from Ron Smillie was handled by a Leicester defender and it looked a certain penalty, but Mr Kelly shook his head. However in that vital moment Ken Oliver slammed a vicious first time shot past Banks and into the roof of the net for the equaliser.

Barnsley were back in the game they would have taken control of, if they had cashed in on their early superiority.

Half-time: Barnsley 1 Leicester City 1

In the second half the game was developing into a battle of defences, with Leicester trying desperately to find a way through Barnsley's resourceful rearguard, and Barnsley striving hard to discover the answer to Leicester's compact defensive wall.

The ball went backwards and forwards from mid-way in one half of the field to the other, although it must be said the ball spent more of the last 20 minutes of ordinary time in Barnsley's half than Leicester's. Indeed there would have been no extra-time if Colin Swift , the Barnsley right back hadn't been on the goal line to head clear a Willis header.

Full-time: Barnsley 1 Leicester City 1

For the first time in their long and memorable Cup run, Barnsley appeared to have shot their bolt, although there were signs of revival in the first period of extra time. However, it wasn't by speed that Leicester took the upper hand as much as craft.

But the match could have gone either way, until the Barnsley defence literally sprang a leak when the match was 107 minutes old. Out on Leicester's left flank, Colin Swift had the misfortune to slip down and former Rotherham player, Ken Keyworth seized his chance. He pinpointed the ball into the middle, goalkeeper Don Leeson hesitated and did not come for the cross, and centre forward Ken

Leek made the best of his only opportunity of the match (he had been completely outplayed by Duncan Sharp) and headed into the net.

Barnsley moved Sharp to the centre forward position, but Leicester's resilient defence held out, and the Reds' glorious Cup run had come to an end.

Result: Barnsley 1 Leicester City 2 (after extra time)

Barnsley: Leeson, Swift and Brookes, Wood, Sharp and Houghton, Smillie, Bartlett, Tindill, Oliver and Lunn.
Leicester City: Banks, Chalmers and Norman, McLintock, King and Appleton, Riley, Walsh, Leek, Keyworth and Willis.

Referee: Mr J Kelly (Chorley)

31

Barnsley v Scunthorpe United

6 January 1964

FA Cup Third Round Replay
Oakwell, Barnsley
Attendance: 21,477

Barnsley 3 Scunthorpe United 2
Bryne (2)   Brownsword (2 pens)
O'Hara

In the first game at Scunthorpe, only goals in the last ten minutes from O' Hara and Bryne saved the Reds, but in the replay, Barnsley battled on in great style, and proved once more that at Oakwell, when it comes to the FA Cup, they are a tough nut to crack. The game was uncompromising, with players going down regularly, after powerful tackle followed powerful tackle.

The match however, will long be remembered as the night of penalties. Referee Mr Pickles dished out three, two to Scunthorpe, but whereas the Lincolnshire side took full advantage of theirs, Barnsley threw their chance away.

Cup nerves were evident in the early stages when Brownsword (twice) and Brookes mis-kicked, and although Scunthorpe made the early running, it was Barnsley who should have opened the scoring. The 13th minute certainly proved unlucky for goal grabbing Tony Leighton. George Kerr crossed from the right and as Neale lost the ball, Leighton turned and pounced, and although he had no one to beat but keeper Jones; and was no more than 12 yards out, he sliced the ball wide.

As the match warmed up into a real cut and thrust battle both sides were indebted to interceptions at the final second. First Hemstead robbed O'Hara just as he was going to shoot, and at the other end Brookes did likewise as Hodgson darted in. For most of the opening half this was how play went, first one side then the other springing on to the attack. Neither side could establish complete command, but as half-time approached Barnsley began to show better ideas up front. Scunthorpe were certainly not afraid to shoot, but Lindsey, Hodgson, Wilson, and Horsfield were all well off target. Their best effort came from young Jim Conde who hailed from the Wath area, and who got the centre forwards job in preference to Barry Mahy.

With 29 minutes gone he beat the entire Barnsley defence to a high ball from

Johnny Byrne was one of Barnsley's best ever technical footballers. A gifted player, never to fulfil his potential, but always exciting who, had he been more committed, would have played at a much higher level. In 78 games he scored 21 goals for the Reds.

a Brownsword free kick and his header struck the bar and bounced behind.

Barnsley's reply to this was a great header by O'Hara which Jones saved magnificently, but the outside left was not to be denied and he put Barnsley in front in the 38th minute with yet another great header. Johnny Byrne fed Houghton astutely and the wing half carried the ball about ten yards before crossing to the outside left. O'Hara's header hit the bar and as the ball bounced down, Horsfield kicked clear, but the referee, after confirmation from a linesman, was satisfied the ball had bounced down behind the line.

Half-time: Barnsley 1 Scunthorpe United 0

Barnsley looked set to move into a commanding position in the second minute of the second half when they got their penalty for a foul on Byrne, but O'Hara's shot struck Jones' leg and the situation was cleared.

It was ironic, then, that Scunthorpe should get back into the match with a spot kick. Lawther was up-ended in a goalmouth scramble in the 66th minute and the veteran Brownsword showed O'Hara just how it should be done by sliding the ball past Williamson with the utmost ease. However, three minutes later, one of the innumerable free kicks that the match produced, led to Barnsley going in front for the second time. Sheavills put the ball in the goalmouth from near the right wing corner flag and Brynes glancing header appeared to be deflected off a defender beyond the reach of Jones.

The excitement mounted. Then, suddenly, the crowd and all the players were thunderstruck when Mr Pickles came up with penalty number three. No one appeared to know why it had been given. Barnsley protested strongly, but the referee insisted he had given it for 'pushing' by centre half Eric Winstanley. Brownsword stepped up again and had no trouble finding the net to square the game at 2–2.

Full-time: Barnsley 2 Scunthorpe United 2

With the match now into extra time, Hodgson gave Barnsley a fright in the first minute by shooting wide, and then the Reds took the lead for the third and last time. George Kerr beat off a tigerish tackle by Brownsword and swung the ball into the centre almost nonchalantly where Tony Leighton worked it on to Bryne. The inside left thumped the ball past Jones like a rocket to send the Oakwell crowd wild with delight.

Although Barnsley's attacking options were restricted in the last few minutes, due to an injury to centre forward Leighton, they were not threatened seriously, and triumphantly marched into round four.

Result: Barnsley 3 Scunthorpe United 2 (after extra-time)

Barnsley: Williamson, Hopper and Brookes, Wood, Winstanley and Houghton, Sheavills, Kerr, Leighton, Byrne and O'Hara.
Scunthorpe United: Jones, Hemstead and Brownsword, Lindsey, Neale and Horstead, Crawford, Hodgson, Conde, Lawther and Wilson.

Referee: Mr J Pickles (Stockport)

Season: 1963/64

P	W	L	D	F	A	Pts
46	12	19	15	68	84	39

Division: Three
Position: Twentieth
Manager: Johnny Steele
Top Scorer: Tony Leighton (24) .

32

Chester v Barnsley

4 May 1968

Football League Division Four
Sealand Road, Chester
Attendance: 4,402

Chester 1 Barnsley 1
Loyden   Winstanley

It was an unforgettable day for Barnsley who, needing only a point to ensure promotion after three seasons in the Fourth Division, achieved their aim.

Referee Jones was no pied piper, but his final whistle was the cue for hundreds of the Reds' fans to invade the pitch and surround the players tunnel calling for the name of that unsung hero, manager Johnny Steele.

How ironic that while Barnsley were bringing out the bottles of champagne, Chester, who had not been outshone, and so nearly clinched both points, were only emptying an ink bottle to write their application for re-election. While they went cap in hand to the league, Barnsley wore the crown of success.

On another day Barnsley might have won this match with ease, but they were tense and over anxious and the brilliance of Carling was only one reason why they never reached a stage of superiority, in terms of goals, such as would have removed the nervousness from the Oakwell men's limbs.

It was, therefore, a match one had to experience as a kind of emotional conflict rather than enjoy as an event sorely confined to the skill of football.

Goalkeeper Carling had turned one 30 yard effort from Bradbury over the bar, and the Barnsley inside left was just wide from the resulting corner, but there was little of note until the 24th minute. Then Bob Earnshaw won a corner and, as Carling and Winstanley went up for Hamstead's inswinging kick the ball glanced off the Oakwell skipper's face and shoulder into the net.

Barnsley's joy was short-lived however, for within the minute Loyden had equalised and though Hamstead, Winstanley and Earnshaw went near it was all square at the interval.

Half-time: Chester 1 Barnsley 1

In the second half Hamstead, who had one of his best matches for the Reds, was

Barnsley team, season 1967/68: (back row, left to right) E Brookes, P Howard, J Robson, R Ironside, E Winstanley, B Murray, P Graham; (front row, left to right) R Earnshaw, J Evans, J Bettany, B Taylor, G Hamstead.

twice close with headers, Earnshaw had a shot blocked and Bradbury thought he had scored with a fine long shot until the referee nullified it with an offside decision.

Three times Chester scared Barnsley, but Ironside saved at the second attempt from Singleton. Parker performed a saving act when a hesitant Sutton squandered a gift, and, in the last minute, a Loyden volley curled agonisingly across the face of goal and inches wide of the far post.

Jimmy Robson had another good match and Winstanley was a captain in more than name. Chester, whose play often belied their lowly position, had several stars, not the least being teenager Robinson, who made a big impression on his league debut.

Result: Chester 1 Barnsley 1

Chester: Carling, R Jones, Evans, Turner and Singleton, Sutton and Robinson, L Jones, Loyden, Metcalf and Bennett.
Barnsley: Ironside, Parker, Howard, Winstanley and Murphy, Bettany and Bradbury, Earnshaw, Hobson, Robson and Hamstead.

Referee: Mr I P Jones (Glamorgan)

Comments

Barnsley completed South Yorkshire's biggest success story of the season when they clinched promotion to the Third Division. It marked the end of 13 years in the wilderness, for their last taste of league success was in 1955 when they were Third Division (North) Champions.

What Barnsley had done was little short of a miracle. For some eighteen months ago they were almost killed off by an acute financial crisis, and indeed many had given them up for dead.

Promotion had given some sense of significance to the words of manager Jock Steele and skipper, Eric Winstanley, who had both insisted that the Reds were good enough to go up.

Manager Steele, who as a player was in the Barnsley team that won Third Division (North) title in 1938/39 commented: 'We've waited such a long time for promotion that now it's come it's something of an anti-climax. We've worked hard for what we've got. Our early exit from the Cup was a blessing in disguise, and we've managed to stay in the promotion race to the end because we haven't faltered in the final stretch.'

Steele continued: 'I said three months ago that those who went up would be the ones who finished strongest. Well we've taken 11 out of the last 12 points.'

Eric Winstanley, the 23-year-old captain, said: 'I've waited six years for this. It's the happiest moment of my life. We've deserved it because we've always had a great spirit even when times were hard. The boss has done a great job, but I wouldn't like anyone to forget that we've got one of the best coaches in the league in Norman Rimmington. Norman has done a marvellous job. All the players have tremendous respect for his knowledge and ability as a coach.'

Barnsley remained unbeaten at home throughout the campaign, which was only the second time in their history that they had achieved this feat, the 1933/34 promotion season being the other one.

Season: 1967/68

P	W	L	D	F	A	Pts
46	24	9	13	68	46	61

Division: Four
Position: Second
Manager: Johnny Steele
Top Scorer: Johnny Evans (14)

33

Barnsley v Grimsby Town

8 May 1979

Football League Division Four
Oakwell, Barnsley
Attendance: 21,261

Barnsley 2 Grimsby Town 1
Saunders, Bell   Lester

Not even the mathematical pessimists who had been refusing to concede that Barnsley had clinched promotion at Portsmouth on Saturday could argue about the certainty of Division Three football at Oakwell next season after last night's gala performance.

Derek Bell, who netted 22 goals in 53 games for the Reds, scores that winning goal to clinch promotion to Division Three.

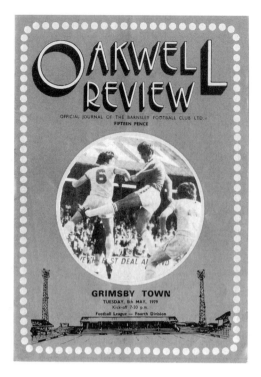

Official matchday programme for the Barnsley v Grimsby Town game.
Barnsley FC

The Reds celebrated in champagne style by producing some of their most exciting football of the season in a marvellously entertaining second half.

For the 21,261 fans who played a big part in making it an occasion never to be forgotten it was the treat of a lifetime, and they were drunk with the sheer pleasure at it all by the end.

But for the brilliance of visiting goalkeeper Nigel Batch, the Reds, surging forward after the break with a power and a purpose which at times threatened to completely overwhelm a fiercely competitive Grimsby side, would have won by at least a four goal margin.

Batch made superb saves from Mick McCarthy, Alistair Millar and Derek Bell, and once he even raced out to the edge of the penalty area to head the ball away as the buccaneering Bell careered goalwards.

Half-time: Barnsley 0 Grimsby Town 0

The game, however, also mirrored the harsh realities of football. For the Reds' first goal, six minutes after half-time, was scored by central defender John Saunders, captain in the absence of player-manager Allan Clarke, who had nevertheless learned at the weekend that in the midst of all the triumph he had been given a free transfer.

What a bitter-sweet moment it must have been for him, as he back-headed Graham Pugh's inswinging corner into the Grimsby net to break the deadlock in what until then, had been a hard-fought, but not particularly exhilarating encounter.

Barnsley players drinking champagne in the dressing room to celebrate promotion: (back row, left to right) Glyn Riley, Gerry Young (coach), Ally Millar, Tommy Graham; (front row, left to right) John Collins, Mick McCarthy, Allan Clarke, Derek Bell, Philip Chambers and Norman Rimmington (physio).

That was the goal which sparked off the period of magnificent attacking football from the Reds, during which the Grimsby goal escaped so many times and the increasingly harassed visitors had two players, Kevin Drinkell and Kevin Moore, booked by a less than satisfactory Wirral referee, Derek Owen.

But then, with only ten minutes left, the Oakwell cheers were momentarily silenced as the Mariners broke away with the speed and directness for which they are rightly noted, and Mike Lester nipped in to slot home the equaliser.

Once again the Reds were faced with a test of character and, thanks to Derek Bell, they came through it with flying colours. Bell, struggling along with bottom of the table Halifax Town seven months ago, scored the winner at Portsmouth on Saturday, and he did the trick again here. He had taken a lot of stick from an over-physical Grimsby defence but did not flinch from the heated action for even a second, typically ensured that he had the last word by netting the winning goal five minutes from time.

He raced on to Millar's defence splitting through ball to notch his 19th goal of the season by smashing the ball past keeper Batch to ensure that the Oakwell celebrations could continue in style.

What a climax to a wonderful campaign for the Boston-born striker, who at £30,000 must be the bargain buy of the season.

Result: Barnsley 2 Grimsby Town 1

Barnsley: Springett, Collins, Saunders, McCarthy and Chambers, Pugh, Little and Millar, Riley, Graham and Bell.

Grimsby Town: Batch, D Moore, K Moore, Wiggington and Crombie, Brolly, Waters, Lester and Cumming, Ford and Drinkell.

Referee: Mr D Owen (Wirral)

Season: 1978/79

P	W	L	D	F	A	Pts
46	24	9	13	73	42	61

Division: Four
Position: Fourth
Manager: Allan Clarke (Player/Manager)
Top Scorer: Derek Bell (18)

Summary of Season

When Allan Clarke was appointed Player/Manager in the summer of 1978, it was his first stab at football management, hence a huge gamble by the Oakwell directors.

However, Clarke immediately made an impact, bringing discipline, organisation, professionalism, and completely revitalised a club that had for the past ten years been going nowhere.

He tinkered a little at first, had the misfortune to lose Brian Joicey to a career ending illness, but waited for the right player before he ventured into the transfer market. He eventually made two crucial signings: Derek Bell from Halifax Town and Tommy Graham from Aston Villa. Both were a success, Bell scored 18 goals and Graham 12, and together with Clarke's 12 ensured enough goals for promotion.

In defence, the outstanding Mick McCarthy confirmed his huge potential as one of the best young centre backs in the country, and in midfield Allan Little provided the drive and determination that at times was almost frightening.

The team got off to a flying start with five straight league wins, and then showed tremendous character in surviving several sticky patches during the season. For those who had doubts that they would make it, the performance at Bournemouth, on the first Saturday in April, confirmed they would be promoted.

The football and commitment that afternoon, on a glue-pot of a pitch, was quite magnificent. Without question it was the best performance of the season, and Clarke and all supporters present, must have been proud to be a 'Red'.

34

Sheffield Wednesday v Barnsley

3 November 1979

Football League Division Three
Hillsborough, Sheffield
Attendance: 23,230

Sheffield Wednesday 0 Barnsley 2
                    Riley, Lester

Barnsley began by playing some neat, quick football from midfield, and they forced Wednesday back when Banks crossed low from the left and goalkeeper Cox did very well to gather the ball at full stretch after Wednesday had been slack when marking from a throw in.

Bobby Flavell then tried a shot from 30 yards, which ended to Cox's left, then Hunter was spoken to after his tackle on Lowey. Wednesday then had a scare from the game's first real threat when, after a long kick down field, Mullen

Mike Lester (not in picture) scores the all-important goal against Sheffield Wednesday to put Barnsley 2-0 in the lead.

Mike Lester was a midfield player who scored 13 goals in 77 appearances during seasons 1978/79 and 1980/81.

impeded Riley inside the area; but from the indirect free kick, Glavin shot wide. After this danger was over, Johnson showed up well for Wednesday with clever work down the right before Pugh dispossessed him, and Barnsley replied with Ronnie Glavin gaining a free kick, but his shot went flashing wide.

After 21 minutes came the game's first booking with Hunter shown the yellow card for not being 10 yards away at a free kick and his name went into the book despite Clarke's protest.

Barnsley, when forced back, had been using Banks as an extra marker on Curran and after 28 minutes when Curran evaded Banks down the right flank, he was brought down by Collins which earned the former Wednesday full-back a booking.

There was a fair bit of tension out on the pitch, but first Clarke and then Pugh provided clever and calm moments for Barnsley before Wednesday hit back with a move which stretched the visitors. Porterfield began the danger by running with the ball from midfield. Lowey played the ball to Johnson and from the full-back's cross, although Hunter did well to beat Fleming in the air, King shot from the left into the side netting.

Fleming did well for Wednesday to gain the side a corner on the left, but when the ball came over, Curran blazed high over. One of the features so far had been the contribution by Glavin for Barnsley from midfield but the side also had bookings to worry about and Banks, required to do a defensive job down the left flank when necessary, became the third player to be shown the yellow card after a trip on King. Wednesday threatened from the free kick, Grant headed the ball across goal, and another header from Mullen, was narrowly over the bar.

Half-time: Sheffield Wednesday 0 Barnsley 0

A shot from Banks from the left flashed across the Wednesday goal, before Wednesday replied with Mullen driving through from defence to cross from the right but Springett held on to the ball.

Then the Reds dramatically changed the course of the game by scoring twice in five minutes to take a firm grip of the action. Riley broke the deadlock when his tenacity paid off to give him an individually worked goal. He showed tremendous persistence and battling qualities and held off a challenge from Grant to shoot low into the net after 48 minutes. Before Wednesday took the kick off, Curran was booked, his sixth of the season. It must have been for something he said, and when the match continued, Lowey almost put Wednesday level following a corner. However, almost immediately, Barnsley rocked the Owls by scoring their second after 53 minutes.

Ronnie Glavin, the most influential player on the pitch, sent Mike Lester through, and with no cover at all, Wednesday were in a terrible mess, and though Cox raced off his line, Lester shot into the net despite an attempt by Grant on the line to clear.

Barnsley and their fans were on top of the world now, and the side built up a superb move which ended with an almost perfect finish when Banks struck a volley not far off target.

The catalogue of bookings continued after 62 minutes with Lester the latest to be shown the yellow card after his tackle on Johnson. A minute earlier Wednesday had brought on substitute Mellor in place of Fleming as they attempted to rescue the game against a buoyant Barnsley team. Wednesday had all on now against determined opponents who that afternoon had the edge over them in all departments.

Barnsley might have increased their lead after 71 minutes when a cross from the right by Clarke was missed by everybody as Riley looked to get a touch at the far post.

The Reds had never given the Owls much time in which to play, and they were now in no mood to let slip a two goal lead. The final whistle came to a chorus of Barnsley cheers, and a first Hillsborough victory for 33 years.

Result: Sheffield Wednesday 0 Barnsley 2

Sheffield Wednesday: Cox, Johnson, Smith, Mullen and Grant, Lemon, Porterfield and King, Curran, Lowey and Fleming.
Barnsley: Springett, Flavell, McCarthy, Hunter and Collins, Glavin, Pugh, Banks and Lester, Clarke and Riley.

Referee: Mr L Robinson (Sutton Coldfield)

Season: 1979/80

P	W	L	D	F	A	Pts
46	16	16	14	53	56	46

Division: Three
Position: Eleventh
Manager: Allan Clarke
Top Scorer: Ronnie Glavin (20)

35

Barnsley v Rotherham United

28 April 1981

Football League Division Three
Oakwell, Barnsley
Attendance: 25,945

Barnsley 1 Rotherham United 0
Glavin

Ronnie Glavin's 15th league goal of the season put Barnsley back in the Second Division, for the first time in 22 years, in front of the Reds' largest home league crowd since January 1953, when they entertained Huddersfield Town.

The first half started nervously on both sides, Rotherham making the first tentative efforts to score. Midfield player John Seasman should have done better in the opening ten minutes with a shooting chance produced for him by overlapping John Breckin.

Shortly afterwards, United keeper Mountford had to be alert and brave to deny Reds striker Derek Parker from opening the scoring and that marked the start of some sustained Barnsley pressure. Almost the whole of one side of Oakwell thought the Reds had gone ahead in the 22nd minute when Barnsley centre back Ian Evans rose to meet a Stewart Barrowclough corner, but the ball flashed just wide of the post. Ronnie Glavin then whipped in a vicious left foot shot that hit Rotherham defender Paul Stancliffe's head, the centre back knowing little or nothing about Glavin's effort.

In the 32nd minute, Oakwell erupted when Glavin scored what proved to be the match winning goal. He controlled a Barrowclough cross, and drilled a venomous half volley towards Rotherham's goal and though Breckin and Stancliffe made valiant efforts to clear the ball from under the bar, both referee and linesman agreed the ball had crossed the line.

Reds midfielder Ian Banks might have made it two, five minutes later, with a clear header from only a yard out, and though Mountford caused more problems for his side by dropping the ball, he should never have been given the chance to save.

Half-time: Barnsley 1 Rotherham United 0

Ronnie Glavin, one of Barnsley's greatest ever players.

Eight minutes into the second half, Ray McHale, who along with Banks, Glavin and Barrowclough had made the Millers midfield look rather ordinary, struck the foot of Mountford's post and was scrambled away to the safety of a corner kick.

Rotherham did win more possession but their strike duo of Fern and Moore were completely snuffed out of the match by Mick McCarthy and Ian Evans, the Reds centre back pair. Indeed, apart from Phil Henson's hopeful hook shot after 68 minutes, which went wildly high, was in fact only Rotherham's second definable shot of the night.

Barnsley meanwhile had to take off a distressed Trevor Aylott after 68 minutes with recurring hamstring trouble, but for an hour or so the wholehearted striker had harassed Rotherham's backline into mistake after mistake.

The late stages produced some frenzied action in the Rotherham goalmouth, but nevertheless the relief was evident all round the ground when referee Richardson blew the final whistle, to send the Oakwell fans into ecstasy.

Result: Barnsley 1 Rotherham United 0

Barnsley: Pierce, Joyce, Evans, McCarthy and Chambers, Glavin, McHale and Banks, Parker, Aylott and Barrowclough. Sub: Riley (for Aylott).
Rotherham United: Mountford, Forrest, Stancliffe, Mullen and Breckin, Towner, Seasman, Rhodes and Henson, Moore and Fern.

Referee: Mr D Richardson (Great Harwood)

The Season's Summary

Despite losing manager Allan Clarke to Leeds United after only six matches into the season, his rebuilt side proved to be the most attractive team in the Third Division, and deserved the success that came to them.

Official matchday programme for the Barnsley v Rotherham United game. Barnsley FC

Highlights of the season were plentiful, a 3–1 away win at Plymouth Argyle in October proved the side quality, and started a sequence of six successive victories. These included a 5–0 thrashing of Hull City at Oakwell, when Aylott scored a hat trick, and a 1–0 win at Portsmouth, who had previously won five games in a row. On 20 December a 2–0 victory over Blackpool extended their unbeaten run to 15 games. A 0–0 Boxing day draw at Chesterfield, a 3 – 0 win over Walsall, in which Ronnie Glavin collected his 99th and 100th goals in Scottish and Football League matches, and a 2–1 defeat of Torquay on 10 January took it to 18 games. The 16 January saw the most dramatic victory of the season at Fulham, when the Reds won 3–2, despite losing goalkeeper Gary Pierce with a serious injury after only six minutes. Sub Glyn Riley took over in goal, but the quality and effort of the performance that Friday evening set the tone for the remainder of the season.

All good teams need a spine down the middle, and that was probably the Reds' success story. Centre backs Ian Evans and the fast maturing Mick McCarthy were arguably the best pair not only in Division Three, but the best outside the First Division.

In midfield, the signing of Ray McHale from Brighton, just before the transfer deadline, proved a master stroke; he dovetailed perfectly with Banks and Glavin.

Ian Banks confirmed the promise of his youth and his powerful shooting saw him score 17 goals during the season, and many were vital late efforts which earned valuable points.

At the sharp end, up front, the tireless and hardworking Trevor Aylott, together with the quick and skilful Derek Parker complemented each other, and although each of them scored only 11 league goals, their efforts deserved many more.

Last, but by no means least, was the mercurial Ronnie Glavin. Eighteen league goals in 37 games from midfield was phenomenal, and his class and all round play made him the outstanding player in the division.

Season: 1980/81

P	W	L	D	F	A	Pts
46	21	8	17	72	45	59

Division: Three
Position: Second
Manager: Norman Hunter
Top Scorer: Ronnie Glavin (18)

Barnsley FC, 1980/81: (back row, left to right) Ian Evans, Trevor Aylott, Martin New, Mick McCarthy; (middle row, left to right) Bobby Collins (coach), Norman Rimmington (physio), Joe Joyce, Mick Lester, Neil Cooper, Ian Banks, Bobby Flavell, Derek Parker, Winston Campbell, Norman Hunter (manager); (front row, left to right) Bobby Downs, Phil Chambers, Ronnie Glavin, Glyn Riley.

36

Barnsley v Brighton & Hove Albion

10 November 1981

Football League Cup Third Round
Oakwell, Barnsley
Attendance: 19,534

Barnsley 4 Brighton & Hove Albion 1
Aylott (2)   Gatting
Glavin, McCarthy

Two months ago, back in September, Barnsley claimed the title of Champion's of South Yorkshire on the strength of a 1–0 win against Sheffield Wednesday. After the complete demolition of First Division Brighton, there can be no doubt that they are the region's team of the moment.

However, there was no indication of the dramatic upset to come as Brighton rather luckily took the lead after only two minutes, when a shot from defender Steve Gatting from 18 yards was deflected past the stranded Bobby Horn.

Many teams would have crumbled going behind so early in the game, particularly to a good first division side. But all that goal did was to ensure the Reds shrugged off the setback and battled their way back into the match, forcing two consecutive corners in the first ten minutes. A minute later, Barnsley were on level terms, Ronnie Glavin back from injury started the move from the halfway line with a flash of his skilful footwork. He fed Ian Banks on the right, whose cross was headed against the post by Trevor Aylott and there was Glavin to touch home the equaliser. It was a break the Reds took full advantage of and Gatting was forced to clear with Aylott threatening, then Parker had a shot held by keeper Graham Mosley. From then on despite a brief spell of some slick one touch football, the seasiders were torn to shreds.

In the 20th minute, Barnsley were in front with a magnificent headed goal by Mick McCarthy. Derek Parker was bundled off the ball by full-back Nelson, who conceded a corner and although there were appeals for a penalty, the home fans were well satisfied when Banks' cross from the flag kick was netted by a bullet header from the outstanding young defender.

In the 35th minute Brighton lost one of their many six figure signings, Andy Ritchie, but his departure did not have a big bearing on the game. Gary Stevens was an able substitute, but like the other ten Brighton players, had to play second fiddle.

Trevor Aylott (with ball) produced an outstanding exhibition of centre forward play in the Brighton cup-tie. Signed from Chelsea in November 1979, he went on to score 34 goals in 124 appearances before moving to Millwall in August 1962.

Half-time: Barnsley 2 Brighton & Hove Albion 1

The visitors were down, but not quite out when the second half began, but after 56 minutes the end was nigh, when Trevor Aylott scored a truly unbelievable goal. He robbed centre back Steve Foster (the man he had tormented all night) out on the right touchline and in one sweet movement looked up, saw keeper Moseley fractionally off his line and from fully 35 yards lobbed the ball into the top corner of the net.

Four minutes later, Glavin had a debatable goal disallowed for pushing by Aylott, but with the crowd baying for more, the Reds answered with goal number four. Moseley did well to go full length to deny a Derek Parker piledriver, but failed to hang on to the ball, Barrowclough put it back into the middle and Aylott's head added the final nail in Brighton's coffin.

The visitors did try to restore some pride in the closing stages, but were denied by Horn, who made one superb save from Tony Grealish in the last minute which prompted Brighton striker Mick Robinson into generous applause.

Barnsley's performance oozed with individual and collective skills. Bobby Horn made some vital saves, Mick McCarthy completely dominated Republic of Ireland striker Robinson, Ray McHale revelled in his midfield anchor role against his old club to produce arguably his best performance since joining the Reds. Parker led Gatting a merry dance, and Aylott made Steve Foster, strongly backed for an England call-up, look very ordinary indeed.

Result: Barnsley 4 Brighton & Hove Albion 1
Barnsley: Horn, Joyce, Evans, McCarthy and Chambers, Glavin, McHale and Banks, Parker, Aylott and Barrowclough.
Brighton & Hove Albion: Moseley, Shanks, Foster, Gatting and Nelson, Case, Grealish, McNab and Smith, Ritchie and Robinson. Sub: Stevens (for Ritchie)

Referee: Mr G Courtney (Spennymoor, Co Durham)

What the Managers Said

'It was the best exhibition of finishing I've seen for a long time. To go a goal down after only two minutes and then fight back the way we did was tremendous. But I still feel that, at times, we have played better football this season. The goals, and the fact that we were playing First Division opposition, made it something special.'
Barnsley Manager, Norman Hunter.

'The way they knocked the ball about was First Division class. They were brilliant, there was nothing we could have done to stop them, and if they produce that kind of form again, I think Barnsley could beat anybody, especially at Oakwell.'
Brighton Manager, Mike Bailey.

Season: 1981/82

P	W	L	D	F	A	Pts
42	19	13	10	59	41	67

Division: Two
Position: Sixth
Manager: Norman Hunter
Top Scorer: Ian Banks (15)

37

Barnsley v Manchester City

2 December 1981

Football League Cup Fourth Round
Oakwell, Barnsley
Attendance: 33,792

Barnsley 1 Manchester City 0
Aylott

Barnsley claimed their third First Division scalp to reach the quarter-final of the league cup for the first time in the club's history. A magnificently headed goal by centre forward Trevor Aylott ended Manchester City's Wembley dreams, and sent them the same way as Brighton and Swansea.

On a dramatic, memorable and exciting evening, Barnsley's biggest crowd at Oakwell since February 1964 when the Reds entertained Manchester United in a FA Cup fourth round tie, raised a tremendous cheer at the final whistle when the team gathered in the centre of the field to applaud the support that carried them through a tense final 15 minutes.

The commitment of both teams was quite staggering and the game was played at a fast and furious pace throughout, but Barnsley towered above their glamorous opponents in terms of wholehearted endeavour and fighting spirit.

The crowd enjoyed an action packed first half and referee Howard Taylor was as busy as any of the players, booking four players in the space of 20 minutes, and six in all with Ranson, McDonald, Reid and Harford entering the book for City, and Joyce and McCarthy for the Reds.

City manager John Bond had obviously taken note of Barnsley's efforts against Brighton and Swansea and paid the Reds the ultimate compliment of instructing his team to go out and prevent them from playing. His players certainly took his advice to heart. Nick Reid was delegated to do a close marking job on Ronnie Glavin, and the rest of the visitors' defence and midfield took no prisoners. But the Reds refused to be intimidated and they never flinched under the pressure City put on them as a result of such tenacious tactics. They responded by raising the pace even more, and City were lucky to escape with only a single goal defeat.

Barnsley winger Stewart Barrowclough gave cause for hope in the opening minutes when he raced down the left, beating Ranson and Bond but Aylott,

One of the game's star players was the Reds' centre back Mick McCarthy. The local-born defender became a legend at Oakwell in his 8 years there, compiling 314 games and scoring 10 goals. He was transferred to Manchester City in December 1983 and was capped for the Republic of Ireland on 57 occasions.
Stan Plus Two

although taking his cross down on his chest, could not find the room to shoot.

The only corner of the first half gave City an opportunity to break the deadlock, McCarthy heading down Hartford's cross but Reeves collecting the ball in space shot wide of Horn's goal. The most controversial moment of the first half came when Riley battered his way through and was stopped by Tueart, but as the players froze expecting a penalty referee Taylor waved play on.

Barnsley could have been a goal up before the break when City centre back Tommy Caton managed to head clear a rasping drive from Ian Evans after 44 minutes, and goalkeeper Joe Corrigan took two attempts to collect a reply from Ronnie Glavin.

Half-time: Barnsley 0 Manchester City 0

City, without the incisiveness of Trevor Francis, rarely created the kind of chance that was going to beat the Reds. Yet one minute into the second half only a freak rebound stopped them taking the lead. Goalkeeper Bobby Horn got his fingertips to a sudden shot by Tommy Hutchinson and turned the ball against the angle of the far post and crossbar, it then hit the astonished keeper on the side of the head and brushed past the post and out for a corner.

A minute later, the Reds were in front. Midfield general Ray McHale started it off, Joe Joyce and Ian Banks worked a triangular move and from Banks' perfect cross, Aylott left his marker Caton, and leapt to send a bullet of a header past a helpless Corrigan. It was Aylott's 12th goal of the season, a bonus for his sinewy, unrelenting pressure upon a City defence which in the circumstances, did nothing to be ashamed of.

It was simply that City had too much to do, too many red shirts to chase.

When full back Ranson finally learned how to cope with winger Barrowclough, new danger sprang from Barnsley's midfield duo Glavin and Banks.

Manchester City then forced a succession of corners, and Horn did well to save a Boyer header before Aylott almost claimed his second. He turned on a Banks' pass and his drive forced a diving save from Corrigan.

As the final minutes ticked away a desperate City mounted a wave of attacks, but the magnificent Mick McCarthy was rock solid at the heart of a superb back four and looked every inch an England class defender.

After the match, Manchester City manager John Bond stated that the Reds should fear no one on this performance, and at Oakwell, with the support they have, are quite capable of beating anyone in the country.

Result: Barnsley 1 Manchester City 0

Barnsley: Horn, Joyce, Evans, McCarthy and Chambers, Glavin, McHale and Banks, Riley, Aylott and Barrowclough.
Manchester City: Corrigan, Ranson, Bond, Caton and McDonald, Tueart, Reid, Hartford and Hutchinson, Reeves and Boyer.

Referee: Mr H Taylor (Oadby, Leicestershire)

38

Liverpool v Barnsley

12 January 1982

Football League Cup Quarter Final
Anfield, Liverpool
Attendance: 33,707

Liverpool 0 Barnsley 0

The amazing scenes at the end of this rip-roaring cup quarter final at Anfield said it all. Barnsley had silenced the famous kop choir at Anfield and, on their performance, thoroughly deserved another attempt to reach the semi-final of the League Cup.

The players showed the same kind of resilience to the European Cup winners, as the thousands of travelling supporters had illustrated by battling through freezing fog and motorway chaos to reach the match. The kick-off was delayed by 10 minutes to allow fans hit by the severe travelling problems to get into the ground.

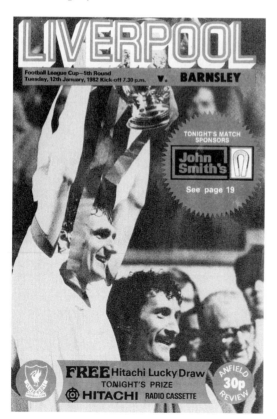

Barnsley, with three First Division scalps in Swansea, Brighton and Manchester City already to their credit, exerted tremendous early pressure and in the first couple of minutes goalkeeper Bruce Grobbelaar had to race out to foil Cooper, deputising for the injured Ronnie Glavin, with Alan Kennedy hooking clear seconds later from Colin Walker.

Official matchday programme for the Liverpool v Barnsley game. Liverpool FC

Ian Evans forged a magnificent partnership with Mick McCarthy in the middle of the Reds' defence and was outstanding in the Anfield tussle. In three years at the club he made 122 appearances, scoring 5 goals.

The tackling was strong and instant, but Dalglish and McDermott got through for shots and then Horn was quickly off his line to frustrate Ian Rush.

In the space of two minutes the Reds forced three corners, one of which resulted in Terry McDermott blocking a goal-bound shot from Ian Banks, with Gobbelaar beaten all ends up. Grobbelaar was caught in no-mans-land shortly afterwards when Ian Evans sent in a header just off target.

Colin Walker, the 23-year-old former dustman, who had the daunting task of making his first full senior appearance, was a revelation. He revelled in the occasion, which was quite remarkable in the circumstances. In fact his surprise debut almost had a fairy-tale ending just before half-time when he sent in a header which brought Grobbalaar's best save of the match, the keeper finger-tipping the ball over the bar.

Half-time: Liverpool 0 Barnsley 0

Barnsley began the second half by creating a series of chances which served as serious evidence of manager Norman Hunter's pre-stated intention of winning on the night. First Walker sent Aylott through, but his effort was blocked by Hansen as Barnsley's newly arrived fans were preparing to acclaim a goal. With only five minutes of the second half gone, Banks was next to grab attention when a half-cleared corner reached him on the edge of the penalty area and he sent back a typical screaming shot which went wide.

A McCarthy challenge on Dalglish saw the ball break to Lawrenson who pushed it wide but Horn beat Whelan to the cross. Walker replied for Barnsley when he beat Neal and Aylott met the cross nicely but headed the ball over the bar. As both sides exchanged alternate attacks, Rush was fouled but Dalglish flighted the free kick wide.

Undoubtedly Liverpool's best move this half was followed by Evans who headed away from Rush after McDermott had latched on to an excellent through ball from Dalglish and sent the effort goalwards.

Bobby Horn followed up his first half acrobatics with a match saving dive when he tipped away a screaming shot from Alan Kennedy.

Make no mistake about it, this was a superb performance by the Reds, particularly taking into account the fact that they were without two of their key players, Derek Parker and Ronnie Glavin, through injury.

It is true to say Liverpool had slightly more of the play, but rarely did they look like breaking down the Reds defence, which was resolute, disciplined and totally unflappable.

When the League Cup holders did manage to snatch a shot on target, they found Bobby Horn in superb form. His handling and positional sense were faultless throughout and he can reflect with pride on his evening's work.

But that of course, applies to all eleven Barnsley players. The back four of Joe Joyce, Ian Evans, Mick McCarthy and Phil Chambers were magnificent.

Neil Cooper came in to do an excellent job in Glavin's mid-field role. While the Reds may have missed the latter's lightning breaks and goal-scoring flair, there is no doubt that his fellow Scot added greater stability and solidity to Barnsley's defensive qualities.

Ian Banks and Ray McHale stifled Liverpool in midfield but also found time to prompt numerous counter-attacks, Stewart Barrowclough worked hard and unselfishly down the left flank, and Trevor Aylott looked the most accomplished player on the pitch.

It was a team performance of the highest order, bursting with pride, skill, character and commitment to match the best Liverpool could offer, and it was a powerful pulsating, gripping contest, which was probably Barnsley's proudest day since the winning of the FA Cup in 1912.

Result: Liverpool 0 Barnsley 0

Liverpool: Grobbelaar, Neale, Thompson, Hansen and Lawrenson, McDermott, Souness, Whelan and Kennedy, Dalglish and Rush.
Barnsley: Horn, Joyce, Evans, McCarthy and Chambers, Cooper, McHale, Banks and Barrowclough, Aylott and Walker.

Referee: Mr D Shaw (Sandbach)

Note

In the replay at Oakwell seven days later, Liverpool won 3–1, after Colin Walker had scored to put the Reds in front.

39

Barnsley v Fulham

2 October 1982

Football League Division Two
Oakwell, Barnsley
Attendance: 12,582

Barnsley 4 Fulham 3
Banks (2)   Hopkins, Wilson, Davies
Glavin,
Cunningham

Barnsley striker Derek Parker shook off what appeared to be an impending bout of flu to line up alongside new signing, Tony Cunningham, who was making his home debut for the Reds.

Before the match, Barnsley's other new signing, midfielder Billy Ronson, received the Hennessy Cognac Player of the Month award for September.

Oakwell, witnessed one of the most sensational starts in Barnsley's long history with four goals in the first 15 minutes, the first three inside seven minutes and all to Fulham.

The first came with less than a minute gone when a poor clearance fell straight at the feet of Hopkins, who promptly planted the ball low into the corner of the net.

Three half-hearted efforts at clearing the ball unnecessarily kept the pressure on Barnsley and it was left to Cunningham to clear when Fulham tried a fourth time. But Cunningham got it all wrong when Fulham put over a free kick from the right. This time, he only half-cleared and Wilson was there to put away another chance for goal number two.

Then in the seventh minute, the Reds were torn apart again. This time Fulham mounted an attack from the left from where Houghton picked out Davies on his own in the middle and like the previous two goals, it was all so easy with the Barnsley defence in tatters.

Barnsley's only answer to the flood of goals was when Cunningham narrowly missed connecting with a Parker centre and then Parker got in a shot which took a deflection.

It could have been four when O'Driscoll got to the by-line and centred, Chambers missed his intended interception, but McCarthy connected and the ball flew only inches wide of Horn's post. To add to Barnsley's woe, Banks had the distinction of becoming the Reds' first booking of the season for an off the ball

Scorer of two goals in the match was midfield ace Ian Banks. Two-footed, with a powerful shot, he scored 51 goals in 307 appearances for the Reds in two spells at the club. He also played for Leicester City, West Bromwich Albion and Rotherham United. Stan Plus Two

incident. But in the 15th minute, the young midfielder made amends when he handed Barnsley a lifeline. He was the victim of a foul on the edge of the area and despite a seven man wall, Banks rifled the free kick into the net for the Reds' first goal.

Barnsley's chief ploy was to cross the ball high to utilise the height advantage of Cunningham and that almost paid off when he won the ball, but it dropped behind the advancing Parker. Then Lock misjudged a bouncing ball and then McCarthy linked up with Ronson to try a 20 yard shot but was off target.

Banks was unfortunate not to get a second goal when he hit a left foot volley that goalkeeper Peyton held at the second attempt.

On the stroke of half-time Cunningham looped a ball high into the area which Peyton misjudged, Glavin got a slight touch but Brown was there to clear.

Half-time: Barnsley 1 Fulham 3

Barnsley won a corner in the opening seconds of the second half and Glavin, via a header from McCarthy, was only a foot away from scoring.

But then, as had happened at the start of the game, Barnsley's defence gave Fulham far too much room. Davies cheekily back heeled onto the roof of the net and in a Fulham counter attack Davies skinned Souter, but Horn got his legs in the way at the expense of a corner.

Cunningham's head was prominent on a couple of occasions as the Reds attacked but twice he failed to find a red shirt with his knock downs.

Fulham keeper Peyton showed remarkable assurance in his own judgment when he allowed a curling centre from Law, now prominent in Barnsley's attacks down the right, go out for a goal kick.

Cunningham then won a corner, and some thought he should have won a penalty, but when it came over, McCarthy headed wide.

The pattern of play was vastly different to the first half. Now Fulham were

144

Ian Banks in action. Stan Plus Two

concentrating a lot more on defence with midfielder Wilson playing just in front of the back four.

That meant the onus was on Barnsley to force the pace and in the 69th minute the Reds pulled another goal back in an highly unusual fashion. Glavin fed Banks on the left and the latter sent in a left-footer that Peyton pushed high into the air but backwards. He looked to have stopped the ball travelling over the line with a dash back and punch out but as play moved out towards the half-way line, the referee looked over to his linesman who signalled that the ball had in fact crossed the line for a goal.

The second booking came shortly afterwards with Hopkins getting his name taken. Four minutes later Barnsley were level. Parker's shot was partially smothered and Glavin ran in to beat Peyton who had been left stranded by the deflection.

Oakwell went into ecstasy three minutes later when Banks centred and Cunningham marked his home debut with a cracking header to complete one of the most amazing fight-backs the Reds crowd has ever seen.

Result: Barnsley 4 Fulham 3

Barnsley: Horn, Law, Souter, McCarthy and Chambers, Glavin, Ronson and Banks, Birch, Parker and Cunningham. Sub: Barrowclough
Fulham: Peyton, Hopkins, O'Driscoll, Gale and Lock, Davies, Brown, Houghton and Lewington, Wilson and Coney. Sub: Parker

Referee: Mr M Robinson (Sutton Coldfield)

Season: 1982/83

P	W	L	D	F	A	Pts
42	14	13	15	57	55	57

Division: Two
Position: Tenth
Manager: Norman Hunter
Top Scorer: Ronnie Glavin (17)

40

Sheffield United v Barnsley

9 November 1982

Football League Cup Third Round (Milk Cup)
Bramall Lane, Sheffield
Attendance: 25,207

Sheffield United 1 Barnsley 3
Edwards   Glavin (2), Kenworthy (og)

Goal ace Ronnie Glavin blasted Barnsley into the fourth round of the league cup at Bramall Lane, when the difference in class was very much in evidence.

Yet so well did Third Division United defend that it was not until the last few minutes that the Reds were able to convert their superior technical skills into victory. The fact that the Reds did not put the Blades to sleep long before they did, clearly emphasises their need for a quality striker to play alongside Derek Parker.

However, while they have a player like Ronnie Glavin capable of surging through to score goals from midfield, even that deficiency is not as serious as it might otherwise be.

On this occasion Glavin was involved in all three goals and without his vital contribution, despite the fact that they were by far the better side, Barnsley might well have been shown the exit door.

As it was, they had to fight back after the shock of conceding a well worked United goal in the 22nd minute. Bob Hatton crossed from the left, Mike Trusson headed down and Keith Edwards provided the perfect finish to a copybook move. At the same time the Reds had good reason to feel a little aggrieved because full-back Joe Joyce was still on his way back to his position after being spoken to by the referee, when Mr Tyldesley allowed United to go ahead with a quickly taken free kick after the home team took full advantage of the situation, Hatton using the free space on the flank to good effect.

United put in the tackles, fair and foul, fierce and fast. There was no lack of commitment from them, and in Stewart Houston, picking up the pieces at the back, they had the outstanding defensive player.

Gradually the Reds, taking total control of midfield, began to knock the ball about in real style, with Alan Birch revelling in the freedom he was surprisingly given on the right and Winston Campbell was again showing delightful skill on

Ronnie Glavin was arguably the Reds' most popular player in the last 30 years. The midfield maestro scored 92 goals in 215 games and captured the hearts of Reds' supporters for five years or so. 'Super Ronnie' was a truly gifted midfield player, and Oakwell will be lucky to see his likes again. Stan Plus Two

the ball, but perhaps lacking that sharpness of mind and eye in goal scoring situations.

Campbell also had the misfortune to be booked after an altercation with Kenworthy. The two players had been having a go at each other from the first minute and Kenworthy often beaten for pace, looked the more guilty. But Campbell committed the cardinal sin of being seen, and the booking took the sting out of the game.

It required a couple of typical long-range efforts from Ian Banks to test the ability of Steve Conroy in the United goal, and when half-time arrived with the home team still holding on to their lead, there must have been niggling doubts in the minds of the army of Barnsley supporters who helped to make the crowd of 25,207, easily the biggest of the night.

Half-time: Sheffield United 1 Barnsley 0

Barnsley's total football flowed even more freely in the second half, and although they left it late, they eventually gained their due reward.

Glavin inevitably stole the spotlight, but no one should overlook the part also played by Derek Parker in all three goals. The first, in the 57th minute, came from a Banks corner which was flicked on by Mick McCarthy and then headed goalwards by Parker for Glavin to ghost on the line and poach the equaliser.

For a brief period United were at last stung into action and they almost regained the lead when Bobby Horn made two excellent saves from Steve Charles and Keith Edwards, and Don Souter, who had a good game, nipped the ball away from Edwards when the latter seemed certain to score. But the Reds survived and countered strongly to book their passage into the fourth round with two goals in the last six minutes.

Hunter took off Campbell, put on another of Oakwell's promising youngsters, Carl Airey, but as everyone was thinking of a replay at Oakwell, the tie was quickly settled. A dreadful mix-up in the United penalty area saw Derek Parker's shot deflected into the net by the unfortunate Tony Kenworthy during a goalmouth scramble, to put the Reds in front for the first time.

If the second goal had a streak of luck about it, the third had class written all over it. Phil Chambers chipped the ball brilliantly inside to Parker, who moved it firmly into the path of the strong running Glavin. The mercurial Scotsman accelerated through to beat Conroy from an acute angle with a rasping drive and thus crown an evening of personal as well as team triumph, with his ninth goal of the season.

The Reds gave United a lesson in the art of playing it simply, quickly and accurately and it was difficult to believe this was the same team as the one which turned in such a poor performance at Ayresome Park three days ago.

Result: Sheffield United 1 Barnsley 3

Sheffield United: Conroy, Atkins, Kenworthy, Houston and Garner, Morris, McHale, Trusson and Charles, Edwards and Hatton.
Barnsley: Horn, Joyce, Souter, McCarthy and Chambers, Glavin, Ronson and Banks, Birch, Parker and Campbell. Sub: Airey (for Campbell).

Referee: Mr P A Tyldesley (Stockport)

41

West Ham United v Barnsley

6 October 1987

Littlewoods, Football League Cup Second Round 2nd Leg
Upton Park, London.
Attendance: 12,403

West Ham United 2 Barnsley 5
Robson, Keen   Agnew (2, 1 pen), Beresford, Lowndes, MacDonald

The tie started all square, as the two teams had fought out a goalless draw at Oakwell in the first leg a fortnight earlier.

Barnsley had the worst possible start when they found themselves a goal down after only two minutes, the Hammers forward Stewart Robson putting the London side in front to give them a flying start.

But Allan Clarke's men recovered their composure to surprise the home team with

some delightful, free-flowing football, and the Hammers were fortunate to survive a series of Barnsley raids. Tom McAllister the West Ham goalkeeper had to dive bravely at the feet of central defender Stuart Gray, save a long-range effort from Paul Futcher and then saved at point-blank range from John Beresford, who perhaps could have done better with his effort. The lively Beresford, revelling in his new striking role as a replacement for the injured Rodger Wylde, was halted only at the last minute with yet another attempt.

With the First Division side hanging on, referee Kelvin Morton gave them precious

John Beresford, the scorer of Barnsley's third goal with a glorious free kick, made 100 appearances for the Reds, scoring 8 goals. The attacking full-back, later starred for Newcastle United before finishing his career at Southampton. Arthur Bower

149

Paul Futcher was one of the most constructive centre-backs to have played for the club. The best player on the pitch against West Ham, he played 267 games in six seasons at Oakwell. A much travelled player, his career also took him to Chester, Derby County, Luton Town, Manchester City, Oldham Arthletic and Grimsby Town. Arthur Bower

breathing space when he awarded a very dubious penalty for a hand ball by Paul Futcher. The experienced central defender was under extreme pressure from Liam Brady and as he tumbled backwards the ball brushed along his arm. The referee blew, hesitated for what seemed an eternity, and then, amid furious Barnsley protests, pointed to the spot. Clive Baker made a great save diving to his right to parry Tony Cottee's spot kick, but Kevin Keen was the first to react to net from the rebound.

The Hammers and their supporters must now have thought that the tie was in the bag, but the Reds had other ideas. Before half-time, John MacDonald missed a good chance, a diving header from the same player brought a superb save from McAlister, who also did well to stop an angled drive from Julien Broddle. Then Gwyn Thomas was inches off target with another good effort, and George Parris cleared a shot off the line, to leave the Reds wondering what they had to do to score.

Half-time: West Ham United 2 Barnsley 0

In the 54th minute, Barnsley were back in the match. Alvin Martin, the Hammers' centre back challenged Stuart Gray for a high ball and, much to the delight and surprise of the Barnsley contingent, Suffolk referee Kelvin Morton decided the West Ham player was guilty of a shove in the back and awarded the Reds a penalty. In the absence of Roger Wylde, Barnsley's regular penalty taker, Steve Agnew accepted the responsibility and he tucked his shot beautifully into the bottom corner of McAlister's net to give the Reds renewed hope.

McAlister then made another excellent save from MacDonald, but Barnsley were in no mood to be denied and in the 71st minute Agnew scored the equaliser. Agnew himself was tripped on the edge of the penalty area, regained his feet and struck a superb 20-yard shot through a hole in the Hammers' wall and into the net.

For a while Barnsley seemed to believe they had done enough. Two-two would have put Barnsley through on away goals, but there was still over a quarter of an hour to go and also the possibility of extra-time. Despite all the West Ham pressure, it was Barnsley who should have clinched it in the last minute when Steve Lowndes was clean through, only to be foiled by McAlister.

Full-time: West Ham United 2 Barnsley 2

Extra-time

Ten minutes into the extra time period, the Hammers' defender Gary Strodder gave away a free kick in an identical position to the one which had produced the Reds second goal, and this time it was John Beresford who curled it gloriously into the top corner of the net to give the Reds the lead for the first time.

Three minutes later a magnificent run by Paul Futcher laid the fourth goal on a plate for a grateful Steve Lowndes, and five minutes into the second half of extra time MacDonald completed the rout by scoring Barnsley's fifth.

To come from behind, and to win in such an exhilarating fashion completed a marvellous team performance, but special mention must be made of the contributions of Paul Futcher and Julian Broddle.

Futcher was by far and away the best player on the pitch, and his class shone through like a beacon, while Broddle, a fourth division player only three weeks ago, teased and tormented Parris to such an extent that the West Ham full back did not know which way to turn.

The Reds, with a perfect sense of timing, had chosen the club's centenary year to put on a performance that was, without doubt, one of the most memorable in their long and chequered history.

Result: West Ham United 2 Barnsley 5

West Ham United: McAlister, Parris, Martin, McQueen and Strodder, War, Keen, Ince and Brady, Cottee and Robson. Sub: Dickens (for McQueen), Hilton (for Ince).
Barnsley: Baker, Joyce, Futcher, Gray and Cross, Lowndes, Thomas, Agnew and Broddle, MacDonald and Beresford.

Referee: Mr K Morton (Bury St Edmonds)

Season: 1987/88

P	W	L	D	F	A	Pts
44	15	17	12	61	62	57

Division: Two
Position: Fourteenth
Manager: Allan Clarke
Top Scorer: Steve Lowndes (9)

42

Barnsley v Bradford City

26 April 1997

Football League Division One
Oakwell, Barnsley
Attendance: 18,605

Barnsley 2 Bradford City 0
Wilkinson, Marcelle

Although the game was probably Barnsley's most important league game in its 110 year history, there was a carnival-like atmosphere in the lead up to the kick-off, before a capacity crowd.

Victory of any kind for the Reds would clinch promotion to the top sphere of English football for the first time in the club's history. Long before kick-off,

Clint Marcelle scores Barnsley's second goal to clinch promotion to the Premier League for the first time in the club's history.

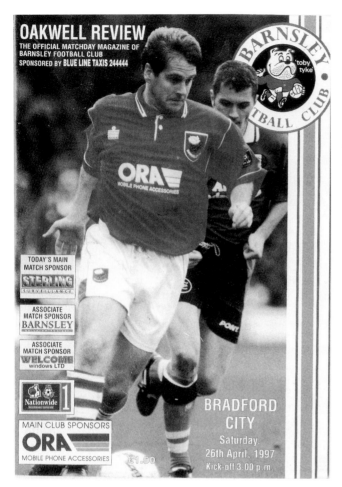

OAKWELL REVIEW
THE OFFICIAL MATCHDAY MAGAZINE OF
BARNSLEY FOOTBALL CLUB
SPONSORED BY BLUE LINE TAXIS 244444

TODAY'S MAIN
MATCH SPONSOR
STERLING
S·U·R·V·E·I·L·L·A·N·C·E

ASSOCIATE
MATCH SPONSOR
BARNSLEY

ASSOCIATE
MATCH SPONSOR
WELCOME
windows LTD

Nationwide 1

MAIN CLUB SPONSORS
ORA
MOBILE PHONE ACCESSORIES

£1.50

BRADFORD
CITY
Saturday,
26th April, 1997
Kick-off 3.00 p.m.

Official matchday programme for Barnsley v Bradford City. Barnsley FC

Player of the Year trophies were awarded. John Hendrie was voted both the Barnsley Player of the Year and the Supporters' Club Player of the Year. Likewise, Adie Moses won both of the Young Player of the Year awards.

Barnsley boss Danny Wilson made two surprise changes from the side which had lost 4–2 at Portsmouth in midweek by giving a start to Andy Liddell and Martin Bullock in an attacking 4 – 4 – 2 formation. Out of the side and on to the sub's bench went midfield player Clint Marcelle and defender Peter Shirtcliff.

The Reds started by immediately laying siege to the Bradford goal and when Bullock forced a corner in the second minute, it was hit long to the edge of the penalty area, where Neil Thompson came charging in unmarked, but unfortunately he missed his kick. Liddell then created space for a cross and Neil Redfearn very nearly got on to the end of it.

But the Valley Paraders weathered the early storm and when Liddell lost possession in midfield, it was City's Robbie Blake, who fired the first shot in anger, from 25 yards, which had the Reds keeper David Watson diving to his right to save. Shortly afterwards striker Mike Newell had a goal-bound effort bravely blocked by Adie Moses, which meant anxious moments for the home fans. At the other end Redfearn forced a corner, Darren Sheridan took it, and Arjan De Zeeuw rose unchallenged but sent his header straight into the hands of goalkeeper Aiden Davidson.

With the game just over ten minutes old, Paul Wilkinson almost put the Reds in front, with a bizarre effort when he charged down a clearance from keeper

153

Davidson and saw the ball drop just inches the wrong side of the post. Liddell then went close again with a brave diving header and closer still with an acrobatic overhead kick which Davidson struggled to palm over the bar for a corner. From then on until the interval, it was a one way procession to the Bradford goal, and during this purple patch the Reds took the lead after 22 minutes. Former City player John Hendrie, despite having a cluster of defenders around him on the by-line, worked his way through down the left and crossed unerringly to find Paul Wilkinson. The Reds striker's glancing header despite having little power, looped up and beyond Davidson's reach to finish into the top corner of the net to send the Oakwell crowd into ecstasy.

Soon Bradford were reeling again when Bullock beat Jacobs to cause pandemonium in the away defence, but somehow City survived. The Reds swarmed forward in search of the vital second goal and City had an even more amazing escape when Redfearn's long-range shot was spilled by Davidson straight to Wilkinson who shot first time, but somehow the keeper managed to block his effort. Again Barnsley pressed forward, Hendrie beat the offside trap and squared the ball for Sheridan who appeared to be impeded just as he was about to shoot, but referee Poulain waved play on. The referee then had to defuse a nasty flare up between defender Dreyer and Wilkinson and when Liburd won a corner, it was Blake's mistake which sent the Reds clear on a counter attack which ended with Bullock setting up Redfearn for another shot from outside the area which Davidson again failed to hold. This time the ball went to Hendrie and once again the Bradford number one made another instinctive block to save his team. But the ball was still in play and went straight to Nicky Eaden who was distraught when he saw his shot thud against the far post and rebound to safety.

Bradford continued to live dangerously and when Hendrie managed to turn in the box his cross was somehow fumbled away for a corner by Davidson. Moses then won a vital header in the box to stop Pepper charging through, but it was still mostly one way traffic towards the City goal.

When Thompson pushed over the Brazilian Edinho on the edge of the Barnsley area, the home fans were relieved to see Murray's shot hit the Barnsley wall and rebound to safety. Newell was booked for scything down Eaden just seconds after he had petulantly kicked the ball out of play after being flagged offside.

Half-time: Barnsley 1 Bradford City 0

Bradford were forced to push forward in search of an equaliser and De Zeeuw gave away a corner, but it was the Dutchman himself who headed clear and the danger was gone.

Hendrie and Bullock combined near the right corner flag to allow Redfearn to fire over from just outside the penalty area. Then the Reds skipper went even

(Left to right) David Watson, Arjan de Zeeuw and Neil Thompson celebrate promotion after the Bradford City game.

closer from a similar range after more good work from Hendrie.

Bradford then took off defender Wilder for their Swedish striker Sundgot, but it was still Barnsley that were doing most of the attacking. Bullock then went on another of his trademark runs and Dreyer was lucky to escape a booking for bringing him down on the edge of the area. Sheridan's free kick hit the wall and the ball was cleared. Bullock then almost surprised Davidson and probably himself as well when his centre almost went straight into the goal. A full-blooded drive from Redfearn was blocked by Pepper and the same player did it again while still lying on the ground when Eaden shot.

On 63 minutes the Reds took off Liddell and brought on centre back Peter Shirtcliff. City forward Surgot then saw his shot beat Watson, but it bobbled inches wide as Barnsley re-grouped into their more usual 3 – 5 – 2 formation, with wing backs Eaden and Thompson pushing forward.

With just 20 minutes to go Clint Marcelle came off the sub's bench for Martin Bullock and immediately Barnsley twice almost doubled their lead. Hendrie used his strength to hold off his challenger and fired in a shot which Davidson did brilliantly to block and seconds later it was Hendrie again, this time on the other side of the penalty area drilling in a shot which beat Davidson, but hit the post.

On 76 minutes City took off Blake and replaced him with Midgley.

Immediately there was an amazing let off for the Reds when Edinho went on a run and crossed perfectly for the Norwegian International Sundgot who was on his own in front of goal. Inexplicably, with the net gaping, he somehow managed to hit the post and the ball was scrambled away for a corner.

Barnsley's pass and move football had destroyed City for most of the afternoon, but the home fans were biting their finger nails with their side only one goal in front. However, with only three minutes to go, the goal all the home fans wanted finally arrived, and the promotion dream had been turned into reality.

Skipper Neil Redfearn threaded through a precision pass to the quicksilver Marcelle, and the mercurial Caribbean International weaved his way past the last City defender before sliding the ball past Davidson's right hand low into the corner of the net to put the Reds 2–0 up and in dreamland.

Oakwell erupted like never before, but Marcelle was not finished, and he ran through the away defence once more, rounded keeper Davidson but saw his shot stopped on the line by Dreyer.

When the final whistle went, the home fans invaded the pitch and for the next half an hour or so, the ground was a mass of red and white.

For the very first time in their long and proud history, the club had finally achieved their ultimate ambition of pitting their wits against the best clubs in the land.

Result: Barnsley 2 Bradford City 0

Barnsley: Watson, Eaden, Moses, De Zeeuw and Thompson, Liddell, Redfearn, Sheridan and Bullock, Wilkinson and Hendrie. Subs: Shirtcliff (for Liddell) and Marcelle (for Bullock).

Bradford City: Davidson, Liburd, Jacobs, Pepper and Mohan, Wilder, Dreyer and Murray, Blake, Newell and Edinho. Sub's: Sungot (for Wilder) and Midgley (for Blake).

Referee: Mr R Poulain (Huddersfield)

Season: 1996/97

P	W	L	D	F	A	Pts
46	22	10	14	76	55	80

Division: One
Position: Second (Runners-up)
Manager: Danny Wilson
Top Scorer: Neil Redfearn (17)

43

Barnsley v West Ham United

9 August 1997

Premier League
Oakwell, Barnsley
Attendance, 18,667

Barnsley 1 West Ham United 2
Redfearn   Hartson, Lampard

Manager of the Year Danny Wilson named a few surprises in Barnsley's first ever Premiership line up. Led by skipper Neil Redfearn, two of the five summer signings made their league debuts for the club, South African International Eric Tinkler and wing back Darren Barnard, who joined just a few days ago from Second Division Bristol City.

Two of the other foreigners, goalkeeper Lars Leese and record signing, the £1.5 million Macedonian striker Gorgi Hristov, were on the sub's bench. However, there was no place in the squad for Slovenian Ales Krizan, and instead the veteran Peter Shirtcliff started in central defence.

West Ham kicked off and Barnard became the first Barnsley player to get a touch in the Premiership when his block conceded a throw in. In the first few minutes both sides produced neat passing moves and Moses did well to foil Kitson after Shirtcliff had missed his kick in the area.

But it didn't take long for Barnsley to get into their stride and they went

Official matchday programme for Barnsley v West Ham United. Barnsley FC

ahead in sensational style on 9 minutes through 'captain marvel', Neil Redfearn. The move started with Eaden's chip for Redfearn to cross to the far post and West Ham were forced to concede a corner. When the ball was swung over, Bullock set up Eaden to cross for Wilkinson. The big number 9 could only just get his head to the ball, but it fell for the Barnsley skipper to throw himself at it and his header looped past Miklosko's left hand and into the net.

West Ham's reply was a Moncur shot from long range which was easily saved by Watson, and the crowd began their favourite chant, 'It's just like watching Brazil.'

There was more danger for the Londoners when Miklosko allowed Hendrie's curler to carry on its way and it went just wide. Another Eaden cross found Wilkinson at the far post but he could not direct it onto goal and another sweeping move by the Reds began with Redfearn feeding Hendrie, who set up Barnard, but his shot from long range went over the bar.

West Ham's Breaker was shown the yellow card for kicking Wilkinson and Moncur brought down Bullock in full flight, but the referee Wilkie played on to the crowd's disgust and it took a crunching tackle by Tinkler to stop the Hammers from counter-attacking.

Redfearn twice showed he had an appetite for a second goal, first by shooting over the the bar and then with a header which was deflected for a corner. From the corner Shirtcliff came charging in at the back post with Miklosko all at sea, but his header was blocked by a defender.

Lomas went on a charging run through the centre and it took a De Zeeuw tackle to stop him from hitting the target. De Zeeuw then stopped Kitson in full flight and the ball ran loose to Breaker, but Moses made a fine tackle to dispossess him.

A minute before half-time, West Ham won their one and only corner of the first half, which Watson punched away, but the Hammers applied pressure and a mix up between Wilkinson and De Zeeuw gave Reiper a clear chance, but he blazed wide.

Half-time: Barnsley 1 West Ham United 0

West Ham changed Breaker for Lazaridis and they dominated most of the opening exchanges in the second half. In the 53rd minute, West Ham equalised when Potts ran through on the left and found Hartson's head with his cross and the ball bounced into an empty net as Watson had charged off his line to collect it, but he never made it and ended up in no-man's-land.

Barnsley's immediate response was to carve out a great chance for Hendrie after good work from Barnard in the West Ham box, but Miklosko spread his body to block the Scotsman's shot at point blank range.

Barnsley had a lucky escape when Lazaridis went down the left and Watson completely missed his cross but luckily for him so did Hartson.

Neil Redfearn scoring Barnsley's first ever goal in the Premiership. Redfearn was another Oakwell legend and the complete midfield player. With the Reds he scored 83 goals in 338 games, a superb rate for a midfield player. In all he played for 15 different clubs, scoring 198 goals in 981 games.

But within seconds of that the Reds were almost back in front when Miklosko had to come out of his area to head away from Bullock, Hendrie latched on to the loose ball but chipped the ball over the bar with the keeper helpless.

On 62 minutes, Barnsley switched formations by abandoning the wing back system for a 4 – 4 – 2 line up when Marcelle came on for Shirtcliff.

With just over 20 minutes to go Hristov came on for Wilkinson and immediately showed his class by shrugging off two heavy challenges to set up Tinkler for a long-range shot. With 14 minutes to go West Ham struck the killer blow, Frank Lampard, turned in a cross from the speedy Lazaridis to score the winner with virtually his first kick, after replacing Berkovic.

The Reds fought back in the closing stages and in the last minute Hristov stole in at the far post to meet a cross from Darren Barnard only for Miklosko to catch the ball underneath his crossbar.

Result: Barnsley 1 West Ham United 2

Barnsley: Watson, Moses, Shirtcliff and De Zeeuw, Eaden, Tinkler, Bullock,

Redfearn and Barnard, Wilkinson and Hendrie. Subs: Marcelle (for Shirtcliff) Hristov (for Wilkinson) and Liddell (for Bullock)

West Ham United: Miklosko, Breaker, Reiper, Ferdinand and Potts, Lomas, Berkovic, Moncur and Hughes, Kitson and Hartson. Subs: Lazaridis (for Breaker) Lampard (for Berkovic) and Terrier (for Hartson).

Referee: Mr A Wilkie (Chester-Le-Street)

Season: 1997/98

P	W	L	D	F	A	Pts
38	10	23	5	37	82	35

Division: Premier League
Position: Nineteenth
Manager: Danny Wilson
Top Scorer: Neil Redfearn (10)

44

Liverpool v Barnsley

22 November 1997

Premier League
Anfield, Liverpool
Attendance: 41,011

Liverpool 0 Barnsley 1
Ward

Barnsley boss Danny Wilson made five changes to the team which lost 4–1 at Southampton. Goalkeeper David Watson was dropped in favour of Lars Leese, but by far the biggest surprise was the inclusion of striker Ashley Ward who had been suffering from meningitis. Skipper Neil Redfearn also returned after flu, new centre back signing from Sweden, Peter Markstedt was included for his debut and

Darren Barnard came in for Ales Krizan at left back.

Liverpool were without midfielder Paul Ince and top scorer Robbie Fowler, while England hopeful Michael Owen retained his place in the attack.

Barnsley keeper Leese had an early scare after five

Ashley Ward, the scorer of the match-winning goal, was a strong, aggressive forward who arrived at Oakwell from Derby County for £1.3 million in September 1977. For Barnsley he made 61 appearances, scoring 25 goals, before a £4.25 million transfer to Blackburn Rovers in November 1998. It is still the highest fee the Reds have received for a player. Arthur Bower minutes when a mix up between him and Eaden allowed Reidle to press towards the Reds goal, Leese dithered and Eaden eventually rescued the situation when he cleared for a corner.

Reidle and Berger created Liverpool's first real chance after nine minutes when full-back Darren Barnard brought down Berger. Berger's free kick found Reidle at the far post and Leese tipped his header over the bar for a corner.

Sensing the Reds raggedness and vulnerability at the back, Liverpool pressed forward with confidence and in the opening stages of the game at least, it seemed as if Wilson's selection gambles were not going to pay off. Whenever Barnsley found themselves in possession they were denied either space or time on the ball which left them lacking the confidence to play a decent pass.

Andy Liddell and Ward faced a difficult task up front. Every time either of them gained any space they found themselves tightly marked by the Liverpool defence. The first 20 minutes were fast and frenetic, with Liverpool generally on top and at times Barnsley were left snapping at their heels, desperate for a sniff of possession. Good work through the centre by Riedle and Berger created an opening for Owen to run on goal, and though his shot had power, it lacked direction and whistled over the bar.

However, Liverpool's best chance came down the right hand side where Barnsley looked ill at ease. Although Wilson had deployed England U21 defender Adie Moses to monitor the movements of midfielder Steve McManaman, each time he combined with McAteer, Liverpool looked threatening.

Despite all the continued pressure the home team were unable to capitalise and Barnsley took a surprise lead after 36 minutes. Full-back Nicky Eaden hoisted a forward ball to Liddell, and as the latter moved towards goal, Liverpool goalkeeper David James came out of his area in an attempt to deny the striker a chance. Liddell rounded him, clipped a cross back across goal, Liverpool defenders blankly stared at each other as the ball dropped and amid the confusion, Ashley Ward was the quickest to react, tucking the ball into the net as the 3,000 visiting Reds supporters screamed themselves into a frenzy.

If against the run of play, Barnsley's first half lead was not surprising. Whilst midfield play was dazzling, Liverpool simply could not turn their pressure into goals while Barnsley defended as if their lives depended on it.

Half-time: Liverpool 0 Barnsley 1

Before the first minute of the second half had elapsed Barnsley striker Ashley Ward had another half chance. Picking the ball up on the halfway line he surged into the Liverpool box and swung a left foot shot just wide of the post.

Barnsley skipper Neil Redfearn saved his side just two minutes later when a defensive mix up left Michael Owen chasing in on goal, and only Redfearn's outstretched leg saved the Reds from conceding an equaliser.

Liverpool pressed forward relentlessly, and nearly grabbed an equaliser after 55 minutes. It was difficult to see how the ball stayed out of the net after good work by Leonhardsen and Owen had bewildered the Barnsley defence. Only Darren Barnard had the presence of mind to clear the ball away from the area.

Liverpool were enjoying the bulk of possession and launched raid after raid on the Barnsley goal, but the Reds were battling for all their worth. Indeed there was simply no way through a superbly organised and tight defence and Liverpool were now showing more and more frustration, and committed several petty fouls, which stopped the flow of the game and played right into the hands of the Barnsley back-five.

When the final whistle came, there was much jubilation in the Barnsley camp, and their superb teamwork, organisation and 100 per cent effort by every red shirt, had justified a magnificent and unexpected win.

Whilst it would be unfair to pick out individuals in what was a team victory, special mention must be made of the efforts of Lars Leese, who made many breathtaking saves, as the Reds last line of defence. Also Peter Markstedt at centre back, who on his debut showed calmness and authority and dovetailed brilliantly with Arjan De Zeeuw in the middle of the defence, and last but not least Ashley Ward who not only ran himself into the ground in the team cause, but also scored the winning goal.

Liverpool 0 Barnsley 1

Liverpool: James, Kvarme, McAteer, Matteo and Bjornebye, McManaman, Redknapp, Leonardsen and Berger, Owen and Riedle. Sub: Murphy (for Bjornebye).

Barnsley: Leese, Moses, Markstedt and De Zeeuw, Eaden, Tinkler, Bullock, Redfearn and Barnard, Liddell and Ward, Sub: Appleby (for Liddell) and Hendrie (for Ward).

Referee: Mr J Winter (Middlesbrough)

45

Barnsley v Tottenham Hotspur

4 February 1998

FA Cup Fourth Round Replay
Oakwell, Barnsley
Attendance: 18,220

Barnsley 3 Tottenham Hotspur 1
Ward, Redfearn,   Ginola
Barnard

Barnsley made changes from the 1–1 draw at White Hart Lane, with Bosancic, Morgan and Bullock taking the places of Sheridan, Marcelle and Tinkler.

The Reds started the match by nearly taking the lead in the second minute when Arjan De Zeeuw headed just wide, then keeper Espen Baardsen saved from Martin Bullock. At the other end Les Ferdinand should have done better when he had a clear chance, but he directed his header straight at David Watson. Then Ward sent a header just wide with Baardsen beaten, before Berti squandered the best opportunity of the half by firing straight at Watson. Hendrie was just too high with one effort and Ginola saw a volley well stopped by Watson, and the half ended with Eaden blazing wide from a good position.

The fact that the first half had remained goal-less was a real mystery as it had been nothing short of a procession of chances at both ends.

Half-time: Barnsley 0 Tottenhan Hotspur 0

Within five minutes of the restart the match was turned on its head with a controversial decision by referee Gerald Ashby. Young Spurs defender Steven Clemence cut inside full-back Nicky Eaden and into the penalty area. Adie Moses barred his way but it looked like Clemence had been unfairly impeded as he hit the floor. All of Oakwell expected a penalty and indeed referee Ashby, who was right on the spot, instantly blew his whistle. But it was to penalise Clemence for attempting to con him with a dive, and as the 19 year old had been booked in the first half, he was sent off the pitch.

While Tottenham's ten men tried to re-group, Barnsley broke down the left for skipper Neil Redfearn to deliver an inch perfect left foot cross which was headed powerfully home by Ashley Ward. That strike transformed the match from an

Barnsley's third goal was an amazing strike from full-back Darren Barnard. He joined the Reds from Bristol City in August 1977 for £750,000 and his sweet left foot gained him 37 goals in 201 games, a good return for a primarily defensive player.

intriguing and well balanced contest into a raging end to end game with attackers often outnumbering defenders in a frantic search for a goal. That was admirably illustrated by Barnsley's second strike, which was the end product of the second significant moment.

Spurs were inches away from an equaliser when Sol Campbell powered past Eaden and rolled the ball across goal to the far post where somehow Jurgen Klinsmann continued to get only the faintest of touches. Yet it was still goal-bound and it needed teenager Chris Morgan, back in the side as one of three centre backs at the expense of Darren Sheriden in midfield, to heroically clear the ball off the line. Martin Bullock picked up the clearance from the halfway line and weaved his way through the undermanned Tottenham defence and although Espen Baardsen saved his initial shot, he was then able to roll it back into the path of Neil Redfearn to hammer home his 10th goal of the season. It could, therefore, have been 1–1, instead it was 2–0 to the Reds and it was now such a significant lead against ten men that Spurs would have needed a miracle to get back into the match.

Shortly afterwards, Ashley Ward looked to have ended all remaining doubts as to the outcome when he swept the ball into the net after Bullock had yet again weaved his way through a desperately retreating Spurs defence, only for the goal to be ruled offside. Darren Barnard then sent a 25 yard shot thumping back into play off a post.

Tottenham were teetering on the brink of a right hammering at this point, but were back in the game when David Ginola, their best player by a mile, netted straight from a free-kick with more than a quarter of an hour to go.

Redfearn and Bullock both missed chances to seal it as Spurs threw men forward, including centre back Raman Vega, but as the match moved towards injury time, Darren Barnard provided the icing on the cake with a magnificent left foot effort which fairly rocketed into the top corner of the net, after the wing back had been screaming from the wide open spaces on the left. Neil Redfearn had thus been involved in all three goals, so his important contribution to a memorable victory was crystal clear.

But there was several outstanding performances within what was essentially an all round team triumph. David Watson, for example, made vital first half saves from Les Ferdinand, Ginola and Nicola Berti, when a breakthrough for the visitors might well have been just the spur they needed. The three centre backs, DeZeeuw, Moses and the no nonsense Morgan dealt superbly with the threat of Ferdinand and Klinsmann, Bullock's bewitching runs had the Spurs defenders in a constant tangle and Ashley Ward was more than a handful for even such an accomplished player as England defender Sol Campbell.

The Reds were all heart and soul, and it was as proud and passionate performance as they had given all season.

Result: Barnsley 3 Tottenham Hotspur 1

Barnsley: Watson, Moses, De Zeeuw and Morgan, Eaden, Bosancic, Bullock, Redfearn and Barnard, Hendrie and Ward.

Tottenham Hotspur: Baardsen, Carr, Vega, Campbell and Wilson, Fox, Clemence, Berti and Ginola, Ferdinand and Klinsmann. Sub: Howells (for Wilson), Armstrong (for Berti) and Brady (for Klinsmann).

Referee: Mr G Ashby (Worcester)

46

Barnsley v Manchester United

25 February 1998

FA Cup Fifth Round Replay
Oakwell, Barnsley
Attendance: 18,655

Barnsley 3 Manchester United 2
Hendrie   Sheringham, Cole
Jones (2)

Barnsley, who were denied a clear-cut penalty seven minutes from the end of the original tie, which ended 1–1, were forced to make four changes from the first encounter. Illness and injury ruled out Nicky Eaden, Alez Krizan and Arjan De Zeeuw and suspension meant Chris Morgan was also on the sidelines.

John Hendrie slots home Barnsley's first goal in the 5th Round Reply at Oakwell. 'Super John' was a huge favourite and a key player in the club's rise to the Premiership. He made 76 appearances, scoring 20 goals, and was appointed player-manager to succeed Danny Wilson. Arthur Bower

United were the first team to dictate the pattern of play, but were rocked on their heels when the Reds took the lead after only nine minutes through super John Hendrie. Darren Barnard chipped a ball over the static United defence for Hendrie to chase. The stocky striker took the ball in his stride and as Peter Schmeichel advanced he produced an audacious finish with a superb outside of the box shot penalty which beat the keeper at the near post.

Eric Nevland had already spurned a great chance for the visitors, lobbing over David Watson but also wide, and when midfield maestro David Beckham's shot hit the inside of the post, spun across the face of goal and out for a goal kick, there was a feeling that this could be Barnsley's night.

Livewire Andy Cole was a constant threat, and he too, should have equalised, but it was by no means all United at this stage. The Reds were closing the opposition down quickly, getting in tackles, chasing and chivvying relentlessly, never giving their illustrious visitors time to settle into their aristocratic stride, and launching some excellent attacks of their own.

United replaced Nevland with Terry Sheringham after 34 minutes, and then a thrilling run from Martin Bullock set up a frantic penalty area scramble, a sweet Ashley Ward, Hendrie, Bullock and Bosancic combination resulted in the latter's shot being deflected for a corner.

In the fourth minute of first half stoppage time after 49 minutes the Reds shocked United rigid by going further in front, when the Lancashire team failed to keep up with the Jones boy. John Hendrie again broke clear, but was crudely brought down by Gary Pallister, a tackle which not only earned the United defender a booking, but at the same time effectively put Hendrie out of the game. However, justice was done because from the free kick the Reds were able to double their advantage, when skipper Neil Redfearn's cross was prodded home by defender Scott Jones as he nipped in unseen in front of the startled Schmeichel.

Half-time: Barnsley 2 Manchester United 0

Andy Liddell replaced the injured John Hendrie and Denis Irwin replaced Brian McClair for United. The Old Trafford team flew at the Reds like wild cats in the second half, Andy Cole fired wide across goal before Sheringham pulled a goal back with more than half an hour to play.

Barnsley had been made to defend much deeper than they were comfortable with and the breaking point came in the 57th minute when defender Peter Markstedt was slow in dealing with Beckham's cross. Cole and Sheringham seemed to have got in each others' way, but luck swung the visitors' way when Sheringham's shot appeared to be covered by keeper Watson, but took a decisive deflection off the unfortunate Moses to end up in the opposite corner of the net.

Barnsley then made a double change, with Clint Marcelle replacing Martin Bullock after 63 minutes and Darren Sheridan coming on for Matt Appleby a

Barnsley players congratulate Scott Jones after he had scored Barnsley's third goal.

minute later. Within 60 seconds the Reds had restored their two goal advantage. Neil Redfearn swung in a right wing corner and Scott Jones rose superbly above Irwin at the far post to thunder home a firm header off the underside of the bar, with Schmeichel stranded in no-mans-land, after colliding with defender Gary Neville.

Ironically, Scott Jones's two goals were his first for the club, and the first goal Barnsley had scored from a corner all season.

It seemed that the night would be theirs but it was the signal for a renewed United onslaught and a fabulous cup tie was back in the melting pot nine minutes from time when Cole made it 3–2 when Sheridan half cleared and Beckham chipped for Sheringham to nod down into Cole's path and the striker gobbled up the chance.

Chances continued to come and go for United, the best falling to Ben Thornley, who hooked his shot over from close range in another mad goalmouth scramble. United immediately replaced Clegg with Twiss after 79 minutes and as the minutes ticked slowly away the referee Mike Riley already public enemy number one in the town because of the first match, somehow managed to find more than six minutes of them after the 90 minute mark had passed.

There was tension all round the ground, but eventually he blew his whistle to a crescendo of noise from the Barnsley supporters, who had just witnessed one of the club's great wins in the history of the FA Cup.

Scott Jones, was the hero of the match with his first ever goals for the club. In five seasons the left-sided defender made 96 appearances for the Reds and scored 7 goals. Arthur Bower

Result: Barnsley 3 Manchester United 2

Barnsley: Watson, Moses, Markstedt and Jones, Appleby, Redfearn, Bullock, Sheridan and Barnard, Hendrie and Ward. Subs: Liddell (for Hendrie), Sheridan (for Appleby) and Marcelle (for Bullock).

Manchester United: Schmeichel, Clegg, May, Pallister and G Neville, Beckham, P Neville, McClair and Thornley, Cole and Nevland. Subs: Sheringham (for Nevland), Irwin (for McClair) and Twiss (for Clegg).

Referee: Mr M Riley (Leeds)

After Match Comments

Barnsley Manager, Danny Wilson: 'That win was one of the best Barnsley Football Club has ever had, and I was very proud of the boys. They fought a magnificent rearguard action at times and earned their good fortune. My heart must have stopped 30 or 40 times in the second half as we came under relentless pressure and maybe luck did smile on us on this occasion, but we are surely entitled to our share after what happened in the first game.

It was a case, at times, of battening down the hatches and getting bodies in the way, but we defended very, very well. We also scored our goals at very good times, John Hendrie gave us an early tonic, Scott Jones notched the second against the run of play just before half-time, and the same player added the third with virtually our first attack of the second half at a time when we were under so much pressure.

Some people had been writing about the weak team that United were putting out, but I shuddered when I saw their starting line up contained all those internationals. They definitely came to win, make no mistake about that. They worked tremendously hard, and full credit to them. It was a fantastic night from our point of view, and no words can describe the appreciation we all felt for the wonderful support from our fans who have been tremendous all season.'

Sky TV Analyst, Andy Gray: 'It was a fantastic achievement by Barnsley in a game which flowed back and forth. There has been a lot of talk about a weak Manchester United side, but they had seven internationals in the starting line up. It was a fabulous cup tie.'

Fulham Manager and TV Pundit, Kevin Keegan: 'There was some controversy over the offside decision, but maybe it was justice after the first game and that penalty incident, and it shouldn't detract anything away from a fantastic finish by John Hendrie. There was still a lot to do but he put it past Schmeichel at his near post. Scott Jones may not be the biggest, but he's certainly the bravest. He caught Manchester United cold twice at set pieces. I don't think Barnsley would cause them trouble like that, but they showed great determination all through.'

47

Barnsley v Huddersfield Town

27 November 1998

Football League Division One
Oakwell, Barnsley
Attendance: 16,648

Barnsley 7 Huddersfield Town 1
Dyer (2),   Facey
Hignett (2)
Tinkler, Ward, Barnard

The first 45 minutes proved to be one of the most exciting ever in the club's history, with the Reds 6–0 up before half time.

Barnsley included their new signing, Craig Hignett (who had spent much of his career at Middlesbrough) and had been bought from Aberdeen for a fee of

£800,000. It proved to be a debut he would remember for the rest of his playing career.

The Reds soon moved into top gear and after only 10 minutes took the lead through Bruce Dyer. Ashley Ward helped on a Darren Barnard corner for the former England U21 forward to make no mistake scoring from point-blank range.

Craig Hignett playing in the hole behind the front two strikers, Ward and Dyer, soon showed why he could add a

Craig Hignett made a stunning debut with two goals, and missed a penalty, which would have given him his hat-trick. A talented forward, Hignett scored 35 goals in 77 appearances and was a fans' favourite in his two years at the club. He was transferred to Blackburn Rovers for £2.25 million in July 2000. Arthur Bower

new dimension to the Reds play, with one off the ball run from midfield that ended with him shooting weakly at keeper Vaeson from a good position. But he made no mistake in the 19th minute when he timed his run to perfection by glancing a header from Eaden's cross into the net.

The third goal in the 26th minute was a soft one as Vaeson let a low Hignett shot from outside the box slip through his fingers and it squeezed under his body into the net. Huddersfield, who had struggled to compete from the start, lost it completely until the break and went four down two minutes later in the 28th minute when Eric Tinkler rose at the near post to glance home a header from Barnard's corner to make it two goals in three minutes. It also triggered off a chorus of *It's just like watching Brazil*, the fans favourite ditty.

Ward was giving centre backs Jackson and Collins all sorts of problems and they could just not cope with his physical presence. Inevitably, it was the Reds striker who notched his 15th goal of the season to make it five.

It came straight after Barnard had been denied by Vaesen's fingertips when he managed to divert a sublime chip on to a post and the keeper was delighted to see the ball bounce back into his arms. But Huddersfield soon squandered possession and when Eaden fed Ward down the inside right channel, the Belgian keeper rashly came off his line and was easily bypassed by Ward for goal number five.

Four minutes later, after 40 minutes, it was 6–0 and it could not have been a better goal for all Sky TV watchers, who must have been thrilled by the Reds' first half performance. Ironically it was scored by Darren Barnard, who could well have spent the evening preparing for a Premiership debut with Southampton. Barnard, valued at £2 million, was wanted by 'Saints' boss David Jones as part of a swap deal involving midfield player Carlton Palmer.

Jones and his Oakwell counterpart John Hendrie had thrashed out an agreement which would have brought the former England midfielder Palmer plus £500,000 to Barnsley in exchange for Barnard. Fortunately for all concerned the deal fell through and Darren remained at Oakwell.

The goal was set up by right back Nicky Eaden who flung over a cross and the Welsh International struck a first time volley with the outside of his left foot, superbly curling the ball into the top left hand corner, way out of the reach of the despairing Huddersfield goalkeeper. The West Yorkshire team trudged off at half-time without a single shot at goal, and many of their fans could be seen disappearing from the ground.

Half-time: Barnsley 6 Huddersfield Town 0

Huddersfield re-appeared in the second half with an extra defender, Gray replacing Richardson. It seemed a strange move for a team already 6–0 down.

In the 55th minute Hignett wasted a wonderful opportunity of making it a debut hat-trick, when he missed a penalty, scooping the ball over the bar.

Seconds later he was substituted by Clint Marcelle, to avoid the worsening of a pulled muscle.

Naturally the game could not continue at the frantic pace of the first half, but the Reds increased their lead to 7–0 in the 70th minute when Bruce Dyer brilliantly took instant control of a neat Eaden pass, turned and whipped in a low shot out of the reach of Vaeson.

Five minutes later Town substitute Delroy Facey gave some cheer to the away fans which were left, when he netted a consolation goal with Barnsley appealing in vain for offside, but it mattered little. Nothing could spoil what had been a night to remember.

The Reds display had been near perfect and their pass and move football was a joy to watch. The midfield had been short of a player who could not only create chances, but have the flair to conjure up goals in support of the strikers. It seemed in Craig Hignett, the Reds had signed the perfect player for this scenario.

Result: Barnsley 7 Huddersfield Town 1

Barnsley: T Bullock, Moses, De Zeeuw and Morgan, Eaden, McClare, Hignett, Tinkler and Barnard. Dyer and Ward. Subs: (Marcelle) for Hignett, Sheridan (for McClare) and M Bullock (for Dyer).

Huddersfield Town: Vaeson, Jenkins, Jackson, Collins and Edwards, Philips, Richardson, Johnson and Barnes, Allison and Stewart. Subs: Gray for (Richardson), Beech (for Barnes) and Facey (for Stewart).

Referee: Mr B Burns (Scarborough)

Season: 1998/99

P	W	L	D	F	A	Pts
46	14	15	17	59	56	59

Division: One
Position: Thirteenth
Manager: John Hendrie
Top scorer: Ashley Ward (12)

48

Birmingham City v Barnsley

17 May 2000

Football League Division One (Play-off Semi-Final 1st Leg)
St Andrews, Birmingham
Attendance: 26,492

Birmingham City 0 Barnsley 4
                    Dyer (2), Shipperley, Hignett

Having finished fourth in the league, the Reds were consigned to the division play-offs for the first time in the club's history, facing fifth placed Birmingham in the first leg of a two legged affair.

Manager Dave Bassett had to make several changes for this vital ninety minutes and surprisingly made a tactical switch as well. He abandoned his favourite 4 – 4 –2 system, and instead went with three centre backs, five in midfield and two up front. At the back he drafted in 19-year-old Keith Brown for his second starting appearance since his transfer from Blackburn Rovers, to play alongside Chris Morgan and Steve Chettle. Nicky Eaden and Darren Barnard took the wing back roles, Matt Appleby, Eric Tinkler and Craig Hignett formed a central midfield three, with Neil Shipperley and Robin Van Der Laan up front.

But the game was over almost before it had begun for Van Der Laan. In under a minute, chasing a ball on the right wing, the Dutchman went down clutching his left knee. Reds physio Mick Tarmy took one look at the injury and called for a stretcher. Reds Manager Dave Bassett left his seat in the stand to supervise the substitution which saw Geoff Thomas take his place in midfield with Hignett pushed up front to partner Shipperley.

The Reds had kicked off in front of more than 3,000 travelling fans and they survived an early corner which Shipperley headed clear. The defensive hero then became the idol of Barnsley's travelling fans with the opening goal in the 11th minute. City centre back Darren Purse attempted to work the ball along the edge of the penalty area but lost possession to Darren Barnard who slotted the ball into the path of Shipperley. The big striker needed no second invitation and swung his boot for a speculative shot, keeper Myhre dived to his right but was helpless as the ball struck the far post before careering in to the net. It was the striker's fifteenth goal of the season and did much to silence an almost packed St Andrews stadium.

Neil Shipperley (in the middle) flanked by Appleby and Eaden, puts the Reds in front. A strong, forceful and much talented centre forward, he joined the Reds in July 1999 for £700,000. He made 88 appearances, scoring 31 goals. He also played for Chelsea, Southampton, Crystal Palace, Sheffield United and Brentford.

Birmingham came back and a Lazaridis run was halted by Nicky Eaden's foul. Referee Halsey immediately reached for the yellow card. In the 21st minute Martin O'Connor's name joined Eaden's name in the book for a very late challenge on Geoff Thomas, who needed immediate treatment and ensured that both captains had now received a caution.

A Birmingham corner kick was delayed as Tinkler received treatment to an ankle injury, but surprisingly the next substitution was not for Tinkler, but Thomas who had failed to run off the injury. In his place Bassett brought on Bruce Dyer, with Hignett dropping back into midfield. The striker had been merely a bit-part player during the season and in recent appearances had been in very poor form. Birmingham's third corner brought their best chance and a brilliant save by the Reds keeper Miller to deny Hughes.

In Barnsley's next attack Shipperley almost gained another clear sight of goal. Hignett's ball to the big striker was of top quality, but Shipperley, under pressure from a couple of defenders, could not control the ball properly.

Birmingham attacked again with Lazaridis making ground on the left, his cross was won by Furlong, but the ball was quickly cleared by Brown. Shipperley was left limping with a dead leg after a fierce but fair challenge from Purse, which needed Dyer to take on more of the foraging, a task he did well in the remaining minutes of the half.

With half-time approaching Barnsley earned their second corner and after moments of pandemonium in the box, Grainger's foul on Appleby produced a free kick which Barnard blasted into the defensive wall. A third Reds corner eventually bounced out to Morgan, but as the young centre back prepared to shoot, Grainger steamed in and fouled him to earn a third yellow card and also another free kick. Barnard elected to shoot and brought a diving save from City keeper Myhre.

Half-time: Birmingham City 0 Barnsley 1

At the beginning of the second half, Birmingham Manager Trevor Francis made an all or nothing decision to send on striker Marcello and Peter Ndlouv for Andrew Johnson and Darren Purse while at the same time switching to a buccaneer 3 – 4 – 3 formation. It was a tactical decision which backfired badly on Francis during the second 45 minutes.

Man-of-the-match, Bruce Dyer scoring Barnsley's third goal, one of 69 goals for the Reds in 204 games, between 1998-2003.

Within three minutes the Blues' hopes were in tatters when Barnsley fully exploited the gaps which appeared in City's fragile defence. In the 48th minute commanding centre back Chris Morgan played a long ball which set Bruce Dyer off on a charge for goal. The super sub swiftly controlled the ball, muscled his way between the strangely hesitant Gary Rowett and David Holdsworth to plant the ball past Thomas Myhre with a coolness that had been lacking from his finishing in recent weeks, and now the home team really was at panic stations.

The Reds fans were in raptures as the midfield trio of Appleby, Tinkler and Hignett continued to control the game. Indeed Birmingham's only effort to talk about in the second half came when a Lazaridis effort was turned over by Miller, and this together with Bryan Hughes' volley, well saved by Miller in the first half were City's only decent attempts on the Barnsley goal.

Appleby's name went into the book for a foul on the lively Ndlouv. Grainger took the free kick but centred harmlessly over Millers' crossbar. The game was interrupted as Marcello was treated for an ankle injury and on the restart there was more depression for the Blues. In the 60th minute, Tinkler supplied a great defence splitting pass from midfield and amazingly again the irrepressible Dyer eluded his marker and it was 3–0 to the Reds as he controlled the ball perfectly to slide it past keeper Myhre for his second goal of the afternoon.

There was even more explosion of noise from the Barnsley contingent in the 69th minute when Dyer eluded his marker to power home a header from Tinkler's free kick, but it died in their throats when the hat-trick strike was ruled out for offside, due to a linesman's flag.

At this point Birmingham were in disarray, although they did try in vain to get on the score-sheet, and Grainger's shot cleared the bar comfortably for the Reds' keeper Miller. The next spell of Birmingham pressure brought Hughes a half chance and as he weighed up his options, Morgan came in with a sliding tackle. The next goal chance however, dropped to Barnsley, and Eaden's centre found Shipperley at the far post, he headed down powerfully, only to see a chance blocked by Myhre on his line.

Amazingly, with only six minutes left, Barnsley made it 4–0 which virtually guaranteed their place at Wembley in the play-off Final.

Man of the match Bruce Dyer continued to torment the City defence and with Francis's men completely throwing caution to the wind in the hope of at least narrowing the gap for the second leg at Oakwell, the former Crystal Palace striker raced clear on the left. He then made a gem of a pass with the outside of his right foot into the path of Craig Hignett, who demonstrated his own finishing ability by firing his shot past Myhre for his 20th goal of the season and in the process sending the Oakwell fans into dreamland.

Indeed in the dying seconds it was inevitably Dyer who had the last word with a spectacular overhead kick that was inches away from completing an amazing nap hand of goals.

Result: Birmingham City 0 Barnsley 4

Birmingham City: Myhre, Rowett, Holdsworth, Purse and M. Johnson, Hughes, O' Connor, Grainger and Lazaridis, A Johnson and Furlong. Subs: Ndlovu (for Purse), Marcello (for M Johnson) and Adebole (for Furlong).

Barnsley: Miller, Morgan, Chettle and Brown, Eaden, Appleby, Hignett, Tinkler and Barnard, Shipperley and Van Der Laan. Subs: Thomas (for Van Der Laan), Dyer (for Thomas) and Barker (for Barnard).

Referee: Mr M Halsey (Hertfordshire)

After Match Comments

Barnsley Manager Dave Bassett was delighted with his side's victory but also surprised by the margin of the win against what he rated as a strong Birmingham team:

'It was an outstanding performance on the day as we had some early problems in losing Robbie Van Der Laan and Geoff Thomas.'

'I never realised that Barnsley had never been to Wembley, so this result is a great performance and puts us within the sight of the twin towers.'

He added: 'Now we just have to complete the job in the second leg.'

In the second leg at Oakwell, Barnsley were beaten 2–1, but marched forward to the Wembley Play of Final, courtesy of a 5–2 aggregate win.

Season: 1999/2000

P	W	L	D	F	A	Pts
46	24	12	10	88	67	82

Division: One
Position: Fourth
Manager: Dave Bassett
Top Scorer: Craig Hignett (19)

49

Barnsley v Ipswich Town

29 May 2000

Football League Division One Play-off Final
Wembley Stadium
Attendance: 73,427

Barnsley 2 Ipswich Town 4
R Wright (og)   Mowbray, Naylor
Hignett (pen)   Stewart, Reuser

For Barnsley's first ever trip to Wembley, and for the club's most important game since their promotion to the premiership, Manager Dave Bassett persisted with the 3 – 5 – 2 formation that had defeated Birmingham City 5–2 in the two legged semi-final affair. John Curtis was preferred to Nicky Eaden in the right wing back role, with Chris Morgan, Steve Chettle and Keith Brown forming the defensive trio, Bruce Dyer gaining selection over Georgi Hristov alongside Neil Shipperley, and Craig Hignett operating in a free role behind the front two captained the side.

In the league encounters, Ipswich had done the double over the Reds to the tune of a 8–1 aggregate score.

Barnsley were cheered on by a following of over 35,000 fans, started the brighter and soon ripped into the Suffolk team with some free-flowing football, which culminated in them taking the lead after only six minutes. Skipper Hignett who had suffered Wembley heartbreak three years earlier when he had been dropped from the Middlesbrough League Cup Final side, took the ball in midfield from Darren Barnard. He advanced towards goal as the town defenders backed off and from just over 30 yards out, the Reds-top scorer fired in an awesome shot, it dipped and swerved to such an extent that it deceived England's third choice goalkeeper Richard Wright, only to crash against the crossbar. As it bounced down, however, it hit the prostrate Wright on the back and rebounded into the net.

It was technically an own goal, which in effect robbed Hignett of his 21st goal of the season, but the Reds supporters cared little for that, their side were in front at Wembley and the ultimate prize of a place in the top tier of English football and a return to the Premiership beckoned.

With Hignett and Appleby in control in midfield, Ipswich were struggling to

Craig Hignett puts the Reds in front after only six minutes.

get a kick and a few minutes later, Wright was forced into a good save low down from Neil Shipperley. Then Hignett curled a shot narrowly wide from outside the penalty area, another goal for the Reds at this point and the Suffolk team would surely have buckled.

However, an injury to star striker David Johnson after 22 minutes proved to be a blessing in disguise for the Suffolk team. He was replaced by Richard Naylor and he instantly started to cause trouble for the Reds defence with his ability in the air. The substitution had given Ipswich an outlet and with Jim Magilton starting to cause problems down the left side of midfield the Barnsley defence started to panic. In the 28th minute due to some slack defending they conceded a needless corner. Having only partially cleared the ball, Magilton took possession, centred deep into the Barnsley box, and veteran defender Tony Mowbray used his physical presence to power home a header past Kevin Miller for the equaliser.

The goal gave Ipswich renewed hope and with Magilton pulling all the strings it was the Reds who were now on the ropes. Magilton's midfield colleagues Jermaine Wright and Matt Holland, began to control the centre of midfield, and six minutes after the goal, Ipswich should have made it 2–1, with the best move of the game so far. The ball flowed delightfully from player to player and it seemed a goal must result until Miller made a good block save from Naylor and last ditch defending by Brown as Stewart closed in for the kill ensured that the danger passed with only a corner conceded.

However, with the clock showing only a minute of normal time to go before the interval, Barnsley had a wonderful opportunity to go back in the lead. Shipperley's flick down sent Hignett on a diagonal run into the box, he was forced wide by keeper Wright and then went tumbling down as the goalkeeper flung himself at the midfielder's feet.

It was a rash decision by Wright, as Hignett was heading away from goal rather than towards it. But he made contact and could have had no complaint, when referee Terry Heilbron, officiating at his last game before retirement, pointed to the spot.

It was tough justice on Ipswich who in the previous fifteen minutes had been the better team, but it turned out to be the defining moment of the match. The Reds penalty expert Darren Barnard, with a 100 per cent record for the Reds from the penalty spot had a wonderful opportunity to demoralise Ipswich, and send them in at half-time crestfallen. Unfortunately his kick lacked power and Wright, diving low to his right, saved easily. Barnard sank to his knees in despair and a glorious opportunity had been missed.

The defining moment of the match: Darren Barnard's first-half injury-time penalty is saved by Ipswich's keeper, Richard Wright, denying the Reds a half-time lead.

Half-time: Barnsley 1 Ipswich Town 1

As the second 45 minutes got under way, the game continued to edge in the way of Ipswich, but shortly after half time Bruce Dyer had an opportunity for the Reds when he miscued an awkward volley following a neat interchange with Hignett.

In the 52nd minute Ipswich took the lead for the first time in the match. Substitute Richard Naylor pounced on to a mistake by Brown after Magilton had hoisted a hopeful ball forward, drew goalkeeper Miller and chipped the ball over him into the net. Naylor was then booked for taking off his shirt in celebration.

Another six minutes and the blue side of Wembley went into party mode when Jamie Clapham crossed from the left, and Marcus Stewart, a £2.5 million signing from Huddersfield, stole in ahead of Brown and headed in number three.

For the Reds it was now a mountain to climb; off came Tinkler to be replaced by Geoff Thomas and shortly afterwards Dyer was substituted, Georgi Hristov taking his place. Nicky Eaden also replaced John Curtis as Dave Bassett went for broke. Suddenly from nowhere the Reds found new reserves of energy, a flashing drive from Barnard was inches off target, Shipperley had a shot saved low down by Wright, and after Naylor had fluffed a golden opportunity to add a fourth for Ipswich the Reds were handed a lifeline. In the 78 minute a second penalty put the result back in the melting pot.

Geoff Thomas made a characteristic run into the penalty area, was brought down by Mowbray as he attempted to cut back inside the defender, and Hignett quick to seize the ball before anyone else could lay hold of it, this time gave Wright no chance from the spot kick.

Ipswich Manager George Burley then hauled off Stewart, to be replaced by Martin Reuser, as Barnsley with a new spring in their step went in search of an equaliser. Five minutes from the end it was nearly 3–3. Hristov had suddenly began to breathe new life into the Reds as the nerves started to creep into the Suffolk team. From a cross from the right, Hristov powered in a header that had goal written all over it, but unfortunately keeper Wright proved why he had made the England squad, by diving to his right to palm out the header, a save that was surely not only the save of the season, but of the decade.

It signalled that Ipswich were not yet home and dry, but, as the board went up to signal five minutes stoppage time, came the goal which finally ended Barnsley's brave challenge. Their all out assault in search of the goal which would provide them with an extra time lifeline left them stretched at the back. When a long ball out of defence fell into the path of Reuser, he kept his nerve and ran on to slam the ball past the advancing Miller for the fourth and final goal.

The Reds had lost, but the game had been the winner. Both sets of fans, Blue and Red behaved impeccably all day. The Reds fans were superb, not only cheering loudly for their crestfallen team, but were very generous in their applause for George Burley's successful Suffolk team.

Result: Barnsley 2 Ipswich Town 4

Barnsley: Miller, Morgan, Chettle and Brown, Curtis, Appleby, Hignett, Tinkler and Barnard, Shipperley and Dyer. Subs: Thomas (for Tinkler), Hristov (for Dyer) and Eaden (for Curtis).
Ipswich Town: R Wright, McGreal, Mowbray, Venus and Croft, J Wright, Holland, Magilton and Clapham, Johnson and Stewart. Subs: Naylor (for Johnson), Reuser (for Stewart) and Wilnis (for J Wright).

Referee: Mr T Heilbron (Newton Aycliffe)

50

Huddersfield Town v Barnsley

15 May 2006

Football League One (Play-off Semi-Final 2nd Leg)
Galpharm Stadium, Huddersfield
Attendance: 19,223

Huddersfield Town 1 Barnsley 3 (Barnsley won 3 - 2 on aggregate)
Worthington   Hayes (pen), Reid,
                    Nardiello

For the second leg of the semi-final tie, Barnsley boss Andy Ritchie made one change from the first leg match at Oakwell, bringing Paul Hayes back into the team for Chris Shuker. Hayes was given a position wide left of midfield, with Martin Devaney switching to the right.

Paul Hayes slots home the penalty, to level the tie at 1-1. K Turner

An electric atmosphere greeted both teams on to the pitch for what was a delayed start of 15 minutes due to the Barnsley supporters' coaches arriving late after being held up by a motorway accident.

Town, leading by a Taylor-Fletcher goal in the closing stages of the first leg at Oakwell, had an opportunity after only seven minutes, but Andy Booth's volley from a Danny Adams cross flew over the bar, much to the relief of keeper Nick Colgan.

Colgan then went full length to keep out a Danny Schofield shot as Huddersfield put the Reds defence under early pressure.

However, McPhail and Howard gradually got a grip in midfield and Marc Richards and Daniel Nardiello combined nicely to set up Devaney on the right, but Town keeper Paul Rachubka blocked his effort.

Town's midfielder Mark Hudson then sent a dangerous ball into the box, but Booth arriving late at the far post failed to get his head to the ball.

Just before the interval the Reds had half a chance to take the lead when Hayes robbed centre-back Nathan Clarke, but his long range shot was easily dealt with by Rachubka.

Half-time: Huddersfield Town 0 Barnsley 0

Twelve minutes into the second half, the game erupted when the Reds took the lead with a penalty, which was hotly disputed by Town.

Paul Haye drifted away from Martin McIntosh to meet Paul Heckinbottom's through ball, but the Town defender pushed Hayes in the back and although the initial contact appeared to be on the edge of the penalty-area, subsequent television replays suggested a penalty which was immediately awarded by referee Chris Foy.

The Reds regular penalty-taker Marc Richards was gathering himself to take the spot-kick when Paul Hayes got off the floor, grabbed the ball shrugging off approaches from Richards and Nardiello and calmly sent Rachubka the wrong way with a near perfect penalty

The tie was now 1–1 on aggregate and Barnsley's sell-out crowd of 3,703 raised the noise levels as their team were now very much back in the match. Indeed a Huddersfield goal seemed the last thing likely to happen until the Reds midfield general, Stephen McPhail made a dreadful mistake. With plenty of time to clear the ball he decided to pass the ball back to keeper Colgan, but the pass was short and Town midfielder Jonathon Worthington beat Colgan to the ball and it rolled agonisingly into the net to give the lead back to Huddersfield. McPhail appeared distraught, as indeed did his colleagues, but five minutes later they were feeling much better when after 70 minutes they took the lead again to put the tie on level terms.

Devaney, having one of his better games for Barnsley, delivered an excellent

Barnsley players celebrate with Paul Reid, after his header had brought the Reds level for the second time. K Turner

right wing corner, Bobby Hassell headed the ball back across goal and skipper Paul Reid buried an excellent header past Rachubka.

Suddenly the Reds were in full flow and eight minutes later the Red and White Army went barmy when they went in front for the second and decisive time in the match.

Stephen McPhail having recovered his composure after the dreadful blunder which had allowed Town to level on aggregate, won a tackle in midfield. Paul Hayes did a clever back heel which sent Brian Howard racing forward. The attacking midfielder let fly with a shot from about 25 yards which keeper Rachubka could only parry, and goal sneak Daniel Nardiello was first to the rebound and sidefooted the ball into the roof of the net.

Town immediately sent McIntosh up front to support Booth, Pawel, Abbott, replaced on-loan David Graham, and Barnsley too sent on their substitutes, Tommy Wright for Marc Richards and Chris Shuker for Nardiello.

Huddersfield threw everything at the Reds and Gary Fletcher-Taylor had half a chance, but scuffed his shot and with it the chance of taking the tie into extra time.

After an agonising four minutes of stoppage time, the referee eventually blew for time, and the Reds were through to their second Play-off Final and their first visit to the Millennium Stadium in Cardiff.

Result: Huddersfield Town 1 Barnsley 3

Huddersfield: Rachubka, Holdsworth, McIntosh, Clarke and Adams, Taylor-Fletcher, Hudson, Worthington and Schofield, Graham and Booth. Subs: Abbott (for Graham) and Brandon (for Hudson).

Barnsley: Colgan, Hassell, Reid, Kay and Heckinbottom, Devaney, McPhail, Howard and Hayes, Nardiello and Richards. Subs: Wright (for Richards) and Shuker (for Nardiello).

Referee: Mr C Foy (St Helens)

51

Barnsley v Swansea City

27 May 2006

Football League One Play-off Final

Millennium Stadium, Cardiff
Attendance: 55,419

Barnsley 2 Swansea City 2 (Barnsley won 4 – 3 on penalties)
Hayes,   Fallon,
Nardiello   Robinson

Andy Ritchie opted for the team that had defeated Huddersfield Town 3–2 in the two-legged semi-final, for the Reds' second ever play-off final.

Swansea settled into an early rhythm and Tudor-Jones had the game's first shot from 25 yards, but it went hopelessly wide. The Reds then created a chance, Ricketts appeared to foul Devaney, but the referee waved play on, but Nardiello

Barnsley players race to Nick Colgan after the keeper had saved to win the trophy for the Reds. K Turner

put his effort wide from 20 yards. Colgan then saved from winger Brittain, but Barnsley had the game's best chance when Howard broke from midfield and although his shot was on target, Swansea keeper Gueret dived and saved at the second attempt.

In the 18th minute Barnsley took the lead against the run of play. A centre from Devaney was only half headed clear by former Reds defender Kevin Austin and it dropped kindly for Paul Hayes to half volley the ball under Gueret at the near post to send the 20,000 Reds fans into raptures. It nearly became 2–0 when Gueret only just managed to turn a Brian Howard effort past his left hand post.

At the other end Barnsley had a real let off after 25 minutes when ex-Red Rory Fallon flicked the ball on, skipper Paul Reid mis-kicked his clearance and Leon Knight raced clear with only Colgan to beat, hit the post. Within two minutes however, the Swans were level. A long free kick by Gary Monk was flicked on by Tudor-Jones for Fallon to hit a spectacular overhead volley that gave Colgan no chance. Minutes later Fallon was again the hero for his team, heading a Stephen McPhail goal bound effort off the line.

The game was fairly even at this stage, but after 40 minutes Swansea went in front due to a horrible mistake from Colgan. Midfielder Andy Robinson took possession from a quick free kick and ran at the Barnsley defence, he eventually cut inside on to his favoured right foot and shot straight at Colgan. Unfortunately Colgan took his eye off the ball and it spun away and into the net to put Swansea 2–1 up.

A Brian Howard effort finished high and wide as Barnsley went in search of an equaliser and then Colgan made a fine save from Robinson minutes before the half-time whistle.

Half-time: Barnsley 1 Swansea City 2

The second half began with Knight firing over the bar for the Swans while McPhail had a long range shot well saved by Gueret. With 57 minutes gone Reds skipper Reid extended a long leg to make a crucial tackle on Knight after good work from Robinson, who had so far been the best player on the pitch. Howard was then fouled on the edge of the penalty area and Daniel Nardiello, seeing a gap in the Swansea wall, curled a brilliant shot wide of keeper Gueret and into the bottom left hand corner to send the Barnsley fans behind the goal into dreamland once again.

The Reds fans upped the noise level as Swansea replaced Knight with the fans' favourite player Lee Trundle, who got the expected rousing reception from the Welsh fans. Despite the goal, it was Swansea who were pressing most and Hassell, who was having a difficult time trying to contain danger man Robinson, made a great defensive header from a cross by Tate.

Barnsley then made two substitutions of their own: Tommy Wright replaced

The Barnsley players celebrate with the Football League Division One Play-off Trophy.
K Turner

Marc Richards and Dale Tonge went on for Brian Howard who was struggling with an injury; Tonge went to full back, with Hassell in midfield.

With less than five minutes to go, Barnsley had a wonderful opportunity to win the match, Devaney created space down the left, then sent in a cross which was met by Reid, who had stayed upfield after a corner. He did everything right directing his header wide of Gueret, but unfortunately the ball bounced too high and went over the Swansea goal.

Full-time: Barnsley 2 Swansea City 2

Extra-time

Shuker having replaced Nardiello on 96 minutes then produced a great effort, beating three players, but delayed his shot and the chance had gone.

Swansea's player of the match Robinson was then substituted by McLeod, who immediately earnt his side a corner, and then a free kick after being fouled by Dale Tonge, which earned Tonge a booking. Swansea attacked again and Akinfenwa looked to be in on goal until Heckinbottom made a timely tackle. In the dying minutes Trundle should have won the game for the Swans, easily beating Kay inside the area, but missed Colgan's goal when it looked easier to score.

Result: Barnsley 2 Swansea City 2

The game was now to be decided by penalties, Swansea won the toss and the spot kicks were to be taken in front of their fans:

Swansea: Trundle scores with low drive, 1–0
Barnsley: Hayes makes it 1 - 1 with a side foot shot.
Swansea: Britton's firm shot makes it 2–1.
Barnsley: Shuker shoots easily past Gueret, 2–2.
Swansea: Akinfenwa shuffles, stops and shoots over the bar 2–2.
Barnsley: Heckinbottom nets a left foot shot, 3–2 to the Reds.
Swansea: Tudor-Jones blasts past Colgan, 3–3.
Barnsley: Kay, confidently shoots past Gueret, 4–3 to Barnsley
Swansea: Tate must score for Swansea, but his side foot shot his saved by Colgan diving to his right, and the Reds have won and are back in the Championship, and Colgan, earlier the villain for his mistake is now the hero of Barnsley.

Barnsley: Colgan, Hassell, Reid, Kay and Heckinbottom, Devaney, McPhail, Howard and Hayes, Nardiello and Richards. Subs: Wright (for Richards), Tonge for Howard and Shuker (for Nardiello).
Swansea: Gueret, Tate, Monk, Austin and Ricketts, Britton, O'Leary, Tudor-Jones and Robinson, Fallon and Knight. Subs: Trundle (for Knight), Akinfenwa (for Fallon) and McLeod (for Robinson).

Referee: Mr L S Mason (Lancashire)

Season: 2005/06

P	W	L	D	F	A	Pts
46	18	10	18	62	44	72

Division: One
Position: Fifth
Manager: Andy Ritchie
Top Scorer: Marc Richards (12)

52

Liverpool v Barnsley

16 February 2008

FA Cup Fifth Round
Anfield, Liverpool
Attendance: 42,449

Liverpool 1 Barnsley 2
Kuyt   Foster, Howard

An injury time winner by Barnsley's skipper Brian Howard sent Liverpool crashing out of the FA Cup and sent 6,000 Reds fans ecstatic. It also meant that the last time the Reds were beaten at Anfield was nearly 50 years ago in the 1958/59 season.

With goalkeeper Heinz Muller injured and sidelined for months, and Tony

Stephen Foster climbs high above the Liverpool defence to head the equaliser in this titanic struggle. K Turner

Warner cup-tied, Barnsley boss Simon Davey had to recruit West Bromwich Albion's third-choice keeper Luke Steele on an emergency loan basis. He was also missing Lewis Nyatanga and Jon Macken, both also cup-tied.

Liverpool left captain Steven Gerrard on the bench and rested Javier Mascherano, Jose Reina and Fernando Torres but still assembled a team full of internationals.

Simon Davey's team had tremendous support, with 6,000 Tykes making themselves heard in the Anfield Road End, with another 3,500 watching the game live on a giant screen back at Oakwell.

In the second minute they were almost celebrating a goal when from Martin Devaney's great cross Istvan Ferenczi's header was blocked by Jamie Carragher. Both John Arne Riise and Lucas saw long range efforts fly wide at the other end and Peter Crouch headed past a post before Kuyt failed to hit the target from Yossi Benayoun's cross. In the 18th minute Crouch went close with an angled effort that Steele needed to be at full-stretch to touch wide.

However, Barnsley had a great chance to open the scoring in the 28th minute when Daniel Nardiello robbed Sammy Hyypia before racing into the box and forcing Liverpool keeper Charles Itandje into a low save to his right. But it was Steele who was in action at the other end a minute later clawing away an 18 yard effort from Xabi Alonso.

With Alonso pulling the strings in midfield, Liverpool pressed forward and Barnsley's resistance was finally broken in the 32nd minute. Alonso swept the ball out to Ryan Babel, who made ground into the penalty area before pulling the ball back for Kuyt to sweep the ball home from six yards.

Steele did well to keep out a Crouch header on the stroke of half-time, but the Reds had competed gamely, and were still in the match.

Half-time: Liverpool 1 Barnsley 0

In the 55th minute Barnsley took off Nardiello and sent on Kayode Odejayi, giving the team more of an aerial threat, and a minute later the Reds hauled themselves level. Martin Devaney launched an excellent cross on the run from the right and defender Stephen Foster rose superbly above Crouch and Carragher at the far post to power a header that Itandje got a hand to, but could not stop it crashing into the net.

Marciano Van Homoet and Jamal Campbell-Ryce were sent on by Davey to replace Rob Kozluck and Diego Leon, but for the next 25 minutes or so Liverpool bombarded the Reds goal.

Benayoun and Crouch had shots cleared off the line in quick succession, then Hyypia had two efforts blocked as Liverpool stormed forward. Lucas saw a header turned onto the bar by Steele, who snaffled the rebound - then made another good save after Benayoun's run and shot.

Skipper Brian Howard drives home the winning goal in the last minute, in front of a disappointed Anfield Kop. K Turner

Harry Kewell replaced Babel before Gerrard was sent on for Lucas after 75 minutes. The England midfielder's first surging run covered 60 yards and won his team a corner.

However, at the other end, Itandje was looking anything but comfortable and was lucky not to concede a penalty when he clattered Odejayi on the edge of the box. Brian Howard then let fly from 25 yards and Itandje did well to palm away the effort.

Kewell had two efforts blocked, then clipped the bar from 25 yards, but most of the noise was coming from the Barnsley contingent.

Steele then made a marvellous save to turn over a Kewell hook shot and Crouch had the ball taken off his foot whilst in the act of shooting. The same thing happened to Kuyt seconds after, with Denis Souza again the defender with the right timing.

Three minutes from time, Carragher was booked, and then in injury time, referee Martin Atkinson turned down a stone-wall penalty in front of the kop when Hyypia's arm sent Howard tumbling. However, justice was done when an incensed Brian Howard picked himself up off the floor, chased back, disposed Alonso, worked his way into the box and drilled a marvellous left-footed shot just inside Itandje's near post to put the Reds 2-1 in the lead.

The Tykes fans erupted, and they had just 30 seconds to wait for the final whistle and confirmation of a famous victory.

Result: Liverpool 1 Barnsley 2

Liverpool: Itandje, Finnan, Carragher, Hyppia and Riise, Benayoun, Alonso, Lucas and Babel, Crouch and Kuyt. Subs: Kewell (for Babel) and Gerrard (for Lucas).
Barnsley: Steele, Hassell, Foster, Souza and Kozluk, Devaney, De Silva, Howard and Leon, Nardiello and Ferenczi. Subs: Odejayi (for Nardiello), Van Homoet (for Kozluk) and Campbell-Ryce (for Leon).

Referee: Mr M Atkinson (West Yorkshire)

After Match Comments

Manager Simon Davey hailed his Barnsley heroes by saying it was the best moment of his football career: 'To come to Anfield, then go a goal behind, to equalise and then win the game in injury time is just wonderful.'

'All the lads worked so hard, Luke Steele on his debut produced a list of world class saves and kept us in the game.'

Skipper Brian Howard who scored the last-ditch winner commented: 'It was a certain penalty, I have seen it since on the TV monitor, and my ankle was grabbed by someone's hand. But fortunately we managed to get the ball back, and when I hit it, I just knew it was going in.'

Season: 2007/8

P	W	L	D	F	A	Pts
46	14	19	13	52	65	55

Division: Championship
Position: Eighteenth
Manager: Simon Davey
Top Scorer: Brian Howard (14)

53

Barnsley v Chelsea

8 March 2008

FA Cup Sixth Round
Oakwell, Barnsley
Attendance: 22,410

Barnsley 1 Chelsea 0
Odejayi

Kayodi Odejayi is hardly a name that rolls of the tongue, but the African-born striker will long be remembered in FA Cup history as the Reds produced another massive shock to send holders Chelsea crashing out. The Nigerian striker, a £200,000 buy from Cheltenham, had found the net only once in 33 appearances, but he scored the most important goal of his career so far to send the Tykes into the semi-finals of the FA Cup for the first time since 1912, the year that Barnsley won the trophy for the only time in their history to date.

Chelsea Manager Avram Grant made six changes to his team that triumphed over Olympiacos in the Champions League, but there was still a star-studded line-up on view. Missing injured were Frank Lampard, Didier Drogba, with Salomon Kalou on the bench and Claude Makele, Paulo Ferreira and Ashley Cole rested. However, Grant was still able to replace them with Michael Essien, Nicolas Anelka, Michael Ballack and Shaun Wright-Phillips, all internationals. The Reds were still without the injured Anderson De-Silva and cup-tied duo Lewin Nyatanga and Jon Macken.

With a sell-out crowd, the fervent Oakwell crowd provided a backdrop of a tremendous atmosphere and if to prove no fear would be shown, Barnsley took the game to their opponents, carving out the opening chance inside three minutes.

The livewire Jamal Campbell-Ryce's through ball found Brian Howard, the Reds captain who had scored the late winner at Anfield. Although Howard's stabbed shot was blocked by Essien, it at least underlined Barnsley's intent that they would not be easy pushovers.

Half-chances followed for Chelsea, interspersed by a number of counter-attacks from the Reds, who were using Cambell-Ryce's pace along with the height and power of strikers Istvan Ferenczi and Kayode Odejayi.

Michael Ballack ballooned the visitors' opportunity over the crossbar,

Kayode Odejayi heads home the winning goal in the 66th minute to knock out multi-million pound Chelsea at the Ponty end, and proves that big men with big hearts can beat big money. K Turner

followed by an edge-of-the-area chip from Joe Cole that easily cleared the woodwork.

Underlining Barnsley's commitment, Rob Kozluk threw his body in front of a Cole drive, and then the former Sheffield United defender also headed up and over his own bar from almost on the goal-line.

Odejayi had two half-chances, but on both occasions his control let him down. Then in the 21st minute Carlo Cudicini was caught napping on the edge of the six-yard box. The Italian goalkeeper made a hash of attempting to trap a backpass from John Terry, allowing Odejayi to thunder in, but he nudged the ball wide.

Then, eight minutes from the interval, Ferenczi should have found the target after latching onto Bobby Hassell's free-kick, but after flicking the ball up with his right foot, his half volley clipped the outside of the post, the Hungarian sank to his knees with his head in his hands as he appreciated he should have done better.

Within a minute, Barnsley were on the attack again as Howard played in Odejayi in the inside right channel, and, although forced wide, he still fired in a powerful shot that forced Cudicini into a save via his legs. At the half-time whistle the Reds received a thunderous applause, for they were marginally the better side in the first 45 minutes.

Half-time: Barnsley 0 Chelsea 0

Perhaps inevitably, Chelsea were quick out of the blocks in the opening 20 minutes of the second period and the Reds were penned back inside their own half, resorting on occasions to desperate, but effective defending.

After weathering the storm, in the 66th minute Barnsley conjured a goal to lift the proverbial roof off Oakwell. Ferenczi fed Martin Devaney on the right, and after a run from Van Homoet pulled away Bridge, the right-winger delivered a piercing cross to the far post. At 6' 2", Odejayi rose in front of the outstretched hands of an hesitant Cudicini to nod home only his second goal of the season into an empty net.

Chelsea poured forward for the equaliser, but not once was Steele forced into a save as a wall of 10 Red shirts protected him.

All the Barnsley players gave 100 per cent commitment, with Bobby Hassell, Denis Souza and Stephen Foster in particular outstanding. At the final whistle as expected, the fans poured onto the pitch to congratulate the 'Super Reds'.

Result: Barnsley 1 Chelsea 0

Barnsley: Steele, Van Homoet, Foster, Souza and Kozluk, Devaney, Hassell, Howard and Campbell-Ryce, Ferenczi and Odejayi. Subs: Togwell (for Devaney) and Coulson (for Odejayi).
Chelsea: Cudicini, Belletti, Carvalho, Terry and Bridge, Wright-Phillips, Essien, and Ballack, J Cole, Anelka and Malouda. Subs: Kalou (for Malouda) and Pizarro (for Belletti).

Referee: Mr S Bennett (Kent)

After Match Comments

Barnsley Manager Simon Davey: 'We have put the magic back in the FA Cup this season and with Chelsea, Manchester United, Liverpool and Arsenal out, who is to say we cannot go on and win it now? On our day, we believe we can beat anyone.'

'To get to Wembley is a fantastic achievement and our supporters deserve it. They have had some barren spells since the club played in the Premier League ten years ago, but days like this show that dreams can still come true.'

Goal-scorer Kayodi Odejayi: 'I am thrilled to score the winning goal and hopefully I have repaid the faith shown in me by the manager. The team were fantastic and our tactics spot on.'

Chelsea Manager Avram Grant: 'We need to congratulate Barnsley. They played very well and showed good spirit. I am very disappointed, but these things happen in football.'

Chelsea Skipper John Terry: 'They played so well and their commitment was unbelievable. I hope they go on and win it the FA Cup now.'

BBC Football Pundit Alan Hansen: 'Barnsley deserved it. I can't recall so many heroes in one team. Their defending was terrific, it was block, block, tackle, tackle. They were absolutely magnificent.'

54

Barnsley v Cardiff City

6 April 2008

FA Cup Semi-Final
Wembley Stadium
Attendance: 82,752

Barnsley 0 Cardiff City 1
      Lesley

For their first FA Cup Semi-Final for 96 years, Barnsley Manager Simon Davey named an unchanged line-up from the one that beat premiership giants Chelsea in the last eight.

Both teams knew that their opponents in the final would be Portsmouth, who had beaten West Bromwich Albion 1-0 the day before.

Barnsley's following of 34,000 fans were soon making their presence felt, but in only the 9th minute their cheers turned to groans when Cardiff took the lead.

Denis Souza, an outstanding figure in the Reds defence all season, could have played the ball back to keeper Luke Steele, but decided to clear the ball himself which eventually went into touch. Cardiff's left back Tony Capaldi produced a long throw-in, which his opposite number on the Barnsley side, Rob Kozluck headed away but unfortunately for Kozluk his effort only fell to City's left-winger Joe Ledley. Ledley set himself up beautifully for the clearance and produced a left foot volley which flew past the diving Steele into the roof of the net, much to the jubilation of the Welsh fans.

Three minutes later the Reds were unlucky not to be level when Kayode Odejayi beat City keeper Peter Enkleman in the air, only for the ball to be cleared off the line by defender Kevin McNaughton.

Almost immediately Barnsley could have scored again when centre-back Souza's header flashed only inches wide of the post, following a corner from the right.

Barnsley were playing the better football and were certainly unlucky to be a goal behind at this stage. However, Cardiff had shown they were dangerous up-front and twice in the space of a few seconds Steele produced an excellent double save, firstly going down quickly to stop Jimmy-Floyd Hasselbank's low shot and then again to smother Trevor Sinclair's follow-up.

In the 22nd minute Kozluk was booked for an unnecessary foul on

The defining moment of the match: Barnsley's big centre forward Kayode Odejayi, with only the goalkeeper to beat, puts his effort wide of goalkeeper Enkleman and blows the chance to bring the Reds level. K Turner

Hasselbank and a minute later right-back Marciano Van Homoet produced a teasing centre but Istvan Ferenczi after out-jumping McNaughton headed wide of the target.

Ferenczi went close again shortly afterwards but Capaldi cleared his effort yards from the goal-line as the Reds continued to press forward in search of an equalising goal.

In the last ten minutes before half-time a cross from right winger Martin Devaney was headed off target by an off-balanced Brian Howard, and then Bobby Hassell and Devaney conspired to fluff a free-kick on the edge of Cardiff's penalty-area.

Half-time: Barnsley 0 Cardiff City 1

Shortly after half-time Cardiff had a wonderful opportunity to increase their lead when Ledley delivered a pin-point cross from the right, for the unmarked Gavin Rae, but the midfielder could only direct his diving header straight at keeper Steele.

The skilful Peter Whittingham, one of City's most gifted players was then booked for a foul on midfielder Howard, as City replaced McNaughton with youngster Aaron Ramsey and then Steven Thompson for Trevor Sinclair.

Simon Davey immediately replaced a disappointing Ferenczi with Michael Coulson after 65 minutes, and a minute later came the defining moment of the match.

With the Reds on top and pressing forward Brian Howard split open the Cardiff defence with a superb through-ball to free centre forward Kayode Odejayi. Odejayi took one touch, then two, and raced clear of the City defenders Roger Johnson and Glenn Loovens. Keeper Peter Enckleman advanced from his goal, but Odejayi with plenty of time and space and the goal at his mercy tried to squeeze the ball into a small gap between Enkleman and the post. He did not even hit the target, for his right-foot shot smashed into the side-netting much to the disappointment of 34,000 travelling fans and many more at home on their TV screens.

The big centre-forward held his head in his hands, knowing full well that he had not only missed the best chance of the match, but had probably cost Barnsley the chance of a place in the final.

Immediately Barnsley replaced winger Devaney with midfielder Diego Leon, but the game's next chance fell to City when Hasselbank was given an opportunity to score on the right edge of the six-yard box, but Bobby Hassell made a superb last-ditch block to deny the former Chelsea forward.

With less than 20 minutes to go and Barnsley pressing forward City's Whittingham sent in a swerving 25 yard shot which narrowly went over goalkeeper Steele's crossbar and then Rae tried to capitalise on a mistake from Denis Souza, but Steele was quickly out of his goal to deny him.

In the 77th minute Stephen McPhail became the second booking for City after a foul on Howard and shortly afterwards Campbell-Ryce was also shown the yellow card to make it 2-2 on cards.

Odejayi then had a chance to go for goal with a far post header, but instead put it back into the six-yard box where it was cleared by Cardiff's best defender on the day Glenn Loovens.

Jacob Butterfield replaced Kozluck for Barnsley and Riccardo Scimeca went on for Hasselbank for City, but the Welshman maintained a tight grip in defence and although Barnsley had been the better passing team for most of the match, the lack of a cutting edge proved their undoing and dreams of an FA Cup appearance petered out as the final whistle brought the game to a finish.

It had been Barnsley's biggest ever attendance in their history. The crowd of 82,752 surpassed the previous highest at a match which came in the 1910 FA Cup Final at Crystal Palace when 77,747 watched Barnsley draw 1-1 with Newcastle United.

Result: Barnsley 0 Cardiff City 1

Barnsley: Steele, Van Homoet, Foster, Souza and Kozluk, Devaney, Hassell,

Howard and Campbell-Ryce, Ferenczi and Odejayi. Subs: Coulson (for Ferenczi), Leon (for Devaney) and Butterfield (for Kozluk).

Cardiff City: Enckleman, McNaughton, Johnson, Loovens and Capaldi, Whittingham, Rae, McPhail and Ledley, Sinclair and Hasslebank. Subs: Ramsey (for McNaughton), Thompson (for Sinclair) and Scimeca (for Hasselbank).

Referee: Mr A Wiley (Staffordshire)

After Match Comments

Barnsley Manager Simon Davey: 'The result is difficult to take. We've come a long way, beaten Liverpool and Chelsea on the way to reach a cup semi-final at Wembley. But we'll bounce back. Everyone should be proud of the players and support staff, for we win as a group and lose as a group, and no one can take away what we have achieved in the competition this season.'

Barnsley Skipper Brain Howard: 'It is hard to take. We've come so far in the competition and I honestly thought we would reach the final. We were probably the better side for long spells in the game but it just wasn't to be. We'll have the memories, but at the moment we are all hurting.'

Cardiff Manager Dave Jones: 'If there had been someone close to him (Odejayi), I would have been screaming "bring him down". I wanted the lad to pass out or die! But he went on and missed. I guess you need a bit of luck to win a semi-final, and we had that bit of luck.'